MARCO ⊕ POLO

Tips

ICELAND

ICELAND
Reykjavik
Norwegian Sea
ATLANTIC
OCEAN
NORWAY
IRELAND GREAT BRITAIN

www.marco-polo.com

SYMBOLS

INSIDER TIP   Insider Tip
★   Highlight
●●●●   Best of ...
↘↗   Scenic view
☺   Responsible travel: fair
              trade principles and the
              environment respected
(*)   Telephone numbers that
              are not toll-free

**PRICE CATEGORIES
HOTELS**

Expensive   over 25,000 ISK

Moderate   15,000–25,000 ISK

Budget   under 15,000 ISK

High-season prices for two
people sharing a double
room, incl. breakfast

**PRICE CATEGORIES
RESTAURANTS**

Expensive   over 4,400

Moderate   2,650–4,40

Budget   under 2,65

Prices are for a main cou
in the evening, drinks no
cluded

On the cover: Paradise for volcano fans and birdwatchers p. 64 | Culture Night in Reykjavík p. 99

CONTENTS

The North → p. 60

The West → p. 68

The Highlands → p. 76

Road atlas → p. 110

DID YOU KNOW?
Timeline → p. 12
Whaling → p. 22
Local specialities → S. 26
Books & Films → S. 58
The Vikings → p. 74
Super jeeps → S. 80
Currency converter → S. 103
Budgeting → S. 105
Weather in Reykjavík → S. 106

MAPS IN THE GUIDEBOOK
(112 A1) Page numbers and coordinates refer to the road atlas
(O) Site/address located off the map. Coordinates are also given for places that are not marked on the road atlas
(U A1) Refers to the map of Reykjavík inside the back cover

INSIDE BACK COVER: PULL-OUT MAP →

PULL-OUT MAP 𝄜
(𝄜 A–B 2–3) Refers to the removable pull-out map
(𝄜 a–b 2–3) Refers to additional inset maps on the pull-out map

The best MARCO POLO Insider Tips

Our top 15 Insider Tips

INSIDER TIP **Icelandic design**

At Kirsuberjatréð in Reykjavík you'll not only find knitted pullovers, but also off-beat creations in felt or organza. Accompany these with elegant necklaces made of bits of hosepipe and pearls (photo, top) → p. 28

INSIDER TIP **Ornithology in stone**

Artworks of a very special nature: the stone eggs by artist Sigurður Guðmundsson in Gleðivík, lined up along the little coast road in all colours and sizes → p. 53

INSIDER TIP **Underwater experience**

Daring divers can plunge deep down between the continental plates in Þingvallavatn → p. 41

INSIDER TIP **Pompeii of the North**

Fascinating excavations on Heimaey: what will be discovered in the houses underneath the ash? Some hope to re-discover long-lost mementoes → p. 44

INSIDER TIP **Quiet and with a view**

The Vínland guest house is functional and tastefully furnished. The place to come for true luxury: peace and quiet and the view of Lögurinn from the terrace → p. 56

INSIDER TIP **One night in August**

Reykjavík on Culture Night is one giant event, with music, readings and firework displays. Every year, the programme swells to include new offerings, so there's always something interesting to discover → p. 99

INSIDER TIP **Close-up on birds**

You can study at leisure the birds which live on and around Mývatn lake in the museum on its banks → p. 64

INSIDER TIP **Glacier in a glass**

American artist Roni Horn has collected glacier water; see for yourself at her Library of Water at Stykkishólmur that there's more to Iceland's ice than meets the eye → p. 73

INSIDER TIP **Winter sport**
Iceland in winter is more than just shopping in Reykjavík – there are a number of great winter-sport venues, too. The wide expanses of the northwest in particular and around Mývatn are ideal for cross-country skiing. If you like things a little faster, hop on a Ski-Doo snowmobile (photo, bottom) → p. 93

INSIDER TIP **On the glacier**
A night in the Kirkjuból hut on Langjökull has its own special appeal. From here, you can walk across the Langjökull glacier, even without special equipment, since it is fairly even and has few crevasses → p. 87

INSIDER TIP **In Gunnar's valley**
The attractive Fljótsdalur valley was the downfall of the heroic figure of Gunnar. So in love with the landscape – from here you have a particularly beautiful view – he remained on his farm and was killed by his enemies. A plaque tells the story → p. 48

INSIDER TIP **Make yourself at home**
Borgarnes B&B is an old house with prettily furnished rooms – friendly atmosphere included. Its proximity to the sea and the large garden are its special bonus points → p. 70

INSIDER TIP **On the subject of seals**
They gaze up at you with their big round eyes. At the Icelandic Seal Centre in Hvammstangi you can find out how and where they live → p. 97

INSIDER TIP **Dream on**
The Atlavík campsite on Lagarfljót lake is a wonderful spot for daydreamers. In the middle of a wood, whose trees are over 100 years old and up to 12m/40ft tall, you'll find plenty of idyllic corners → p. 56

INSIDER TIP **Camping for all**
The Camping Card is ideal for families or couples – and helps to make your Iceland holiday a little cheaper. The list of participating campsites gets longer every year. The card is available via the Internet → p. 103

BEST OF ...

FOR FREE

● *Down on the farm*
The ruins of the 11th-century longhouse *Stöng*, which can be visited for free, give a vivid impression of the size and layout of farms back then. Route 32 is worth a detour on the way to the highlands → p. 50

● *Iceland in bloom*
The *Botanical Garden* in Akureyri is a freely accessible, rambling site and home to all of Iceland's native plants – plus a great many more from elsewhere. From Greenland to the Mediterranean, if it's green and/or bears flowers, it's here → p. 61

● *Sculpture garden*
Einar Jónsson was the country's first sculptor of note, and consequently many of his works are to be found all over the Iceland. You can also admire an interesting selection of them in the garden adjoining his studio, which is permanently open to visitors → p. 35

● *Get pally with the puffins*
To see puffins really close up, you usually have to take an organised boat trip. On the steep coast at *Látrabjarg* the comical cliff-dwellers come up close enough for you to count the rings on their bills – for free (photo) → p. 73

● *What's geothermics all about?*
Get an answer to this question during a free visit to the geothermal power plant *Hellisheiðarvirkjun*. At the visitor centre, various information points with touch-screens take you through the energy-generating process, and you can learn a lot about the region at the same time → p. 47

● *Romantic spot for a dip*
The little pool at *Selárdalur*, which you can visit for free, has a charm all its own. It lies on an idyllic river, and in autumn is lit up by the Northern Lights as well as candles → p. 56

●●●● Dots in guidebook refer to 'Best of ...' tips

ONLY IN ICELAND
Unique experiences

● *Great knits*

The traditional Iceland pullover is an ideal piece of outdoor kit, and at *Víkurprjón* in Vík they have a huge selection of hand-knitted models with the typical pattern around the neck → p. 29

● *Cultural heritage: sagas*

The preserved manuscripts of the Icelandic sagas are considered natural treasures on the Iceland. They are displayed in a specially darkened room in Reykjavík's *Culture House*. Moreover, almost every region of the country has its own heroic figures whose exploits can be tracked back in time → p. 36

● *Environmentally friendly energy*

The Iceland of *Heimaey* is a prime example of how the consequences of nature's menacing power can be turned to man's advantage: the hot lava heats the water; the ruins and excavations are tourist attractions → p. 43

● *Cascading waters*

Iceland is synonymous with waterfalls; there are thousands of them, many marvelled at daily, others completely hidden from view. The finest is probably the fan-shaped *Dynjandi* (The Thundering One), in the northwest (photo) → p. 72

● *Seething earth*

In some places on Iceland the earth's crust is relatively thin, hence the bubbling, hissing and steaming going on everywhere. If there's also an element of sulphur involved, then you're in for an aromatic experience, as at *Námaskarð* near Mývatn → p. 64

● *Warm baths*

As early as the Middle Ages, people had cottoned on to the delights of bathing in warm water. Since the 20th century, natural baths are a ritual in almost every town or village, whereby a cosy chat in a hot pot is an indispensable element. The oldest pot can be looked at – but not used – in *Reykholt* → p. 71

● *Lava deserts*

Iceland is a land of volcanoes which erupt regularly – as we were reminded in 2010. Ash clouds and lava flows are the result. The beautiful lava deserts, for example *Ódáðahraun* in the highlands, have evolved over centuries → p. 81

ONLY IN

BEST OF ...

AND IF IT RAINS?
Activities to brighten your day

● **Under one roof**
A rainy day is an ideal opportunity to do some shopping and perhaps watch a new film in the original. The two shopping malls *Kringlan* and *Smáralind* in Kópavogur have heaps of shops and giant cinemas → p. 37

● **Explore the city by bus**
Buy yourself a *Reykjavík Welcome Card* and take a ride through the city and those districts you perhaps wouldn't normally visit. This is the best way to get to know the capital → p. 40

● **Water from all directions**
Reykjavík not only has the large swimming pool *Laugardalur*, but plenty of others, too. Sitting in a hot pot in the rain or snow is a real treat. Should the breeze around your ears turn chilly, just take a dive → p. 38

● **The magic of the glaciers**
Examination of multi-coloured glacier-water specimens combined with a fine view: both are possible at the 'Library of Water' *Vatnasafn* in Stykkishólmur. It is also invites quiet contemplation – as dreamt up by artist Roni Horn → p. 73

● **Music in church**
During the summer months there are regular lunchtime concerts in the *Hallgrímskirkja* in Reykjavík. The acoustics in the church are outstanding, the pale grey interior pleasantly unfussy (photo) → p. 35

● **A stroll on the beach**
What is probably Iceland's prettiest beach lies to the west of Vík. The water gurgles as it washes over the black lava pebbles, and you can walk for miles. Since you are bound to have your waterproofs with you on your trip to Iceland, this is a good opportunity to try them out → p. 50

RELAX AND CHILL OUT
Take it easy and spoil yourself

● *Heavenly bus tour*
Iceland's comfortable tour buses are perfect if you want to take a trip into the highlands. Just get on board, sit down and day-dream. The countryside transforms itself as the tour guide explains what you can see out of the windows and the clouds pile up into ever-changing formations. It's a shame to have to get off sometimes … → p. 88

● *Into the blue*
The water will carry you at the *Blue Lagoon* – just let yourself drift off, with a suitable drink to hand. If that's not relaxing enough, treat yourself to a massage, visit the sauna or slap on a mud face pack → p. 39

● *A menu with a view*
What an appetizer: Reykjavik and the surrounding countryside gravitate past as you gaze out from the best window seats in the revolving restaurant *Perlan*. The food, too, is excellent, so a visit to this most unusual eatery is worthwhile whichever way you look at it (photo) → p. 36

● *Northern Lights*
If you take a room at the hotel *Rangá,* you can relax in one of the hot pots outside and savour the view of the Hekla and the river Rangá. On the same spot in autumn or winter, you could be treated to the spectacle of the Northern Lights → p. 48

● *Camping in the woods*
A campsite bang in the middle of the forest! In *Hallormstaður* in Atlavík you can pitch your tent under the trees. Sitting out front, you will hear the leaves rustling in the treetops as you look out over the lake. Or just close your eyes and listen to the wind → p. 56

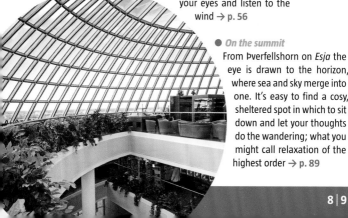

● *On the summit*
From Þverfellshorn on *Esja* the eye is drawn to the horizon, where sea and sky merge into one. It's easy to find a cosy, sheltered spot in which to sit down and let your thoughts do the wandering; what you might call relaxation of the highest order → p. 89

INTRODUCTION

DISCOVER ICELAND!

Iceland is full of contradictions, surprises and secrets. Its archaic volcanic landscape transports you back to the primeval times of the earth's origins. In some places, the earth's crust is dangerously thin, and the bubbling, steaming holes give you a glimpse of our planet's fiery interior. What people in the Middle Ages held to be simply threatening and strange – the work of the Devil and the gateway to Hell – is used by 21st-century Icelanders to great advantage. The lava serves as building material; geothermal energy is transformed into electricity and the hot water heats houses and swimming pools. The Icelanders have learnt how to 'dance on a volcano'. The country's true wealth is its natural resources which are fundamental to the existence of the people who live here. Alongside the power generated from the waters of countless glacial rivers and from the geothermal energy of this volcanic Iceland, it is above all the fishing grounds within the hard-fought 200-mile zone which constitute the Iceland's economic base and which are consequently fished very carefully.

Photo: Seljalandsfoss waterfall

Nature as master builder: fascinating lava formations on the Snæfellsnes peninsula

First and foremost, it is the varied face of the countryside which draws tourists in their thousands every year. In the south, you'll find expansive meadows with broad, black beaches washed by crashing white surf; close by, the black snouts of giant glaciers seem to run out of steam just before reaching the sea. In the east, the steep basalt plateaux surge upwards, into which deep fjords and narrow mountain gorges have cut a path. Wide valleys and the country's longest fjord, the Eyjafjörður, dominate the north.

Black beaches and giant glaciers

The northwest, scored by numerous fjords to form its characteristic jagged coastline, is only sparsely populated. Landslides, which at the very least block a few roads, are common during the harsh winters. The higher ground is a broad lava field scattered with boulders, an inhospitable moonscape of isolated peaks and mountain ranges. Add to this the

874
Ingólfur Arnarson settles permanently in Iceland

930
Founding of the annual national assembly, the Althing, in Þingvellir and declaration of a free and independent Icelandic state

1000
Adoption of Christianity

1262
The Norwegian king is recognised as monarch

1380
Iceland and Norway fall to Denmark

1550
The last Catholic bishop Jón Arnason is beheaded; Den-

hundreds of waterfalls: hidden, thundering, mighty and beautiful – some of them with a tale to tell, others so small you might be the first to stumble across them. All this is concentrated on a single Iceland whose closest neighbours are Greenland (300km/185mi to the northwest) and the Faroe Icelands (500km/310mi to the southeast).

> **The sagas are a national cultural treasure**

The Icelanders love their Iceland and its breathtaking landscape which has formed them just as much as their origins and history. To this day, they still consider themselves the descendants of the Vikings who came here from Norway to live in freedom, away from the then king. First attempts at settlement failed; the Norwegian Flóki thought the terrain too forbidding and icy, prompting him to give it the name Ísland (Iceland). He came ashore in the northwest in 865 AD and stayed just one winter. Only ten years later, however, the Iceland was permanently settled. The next 300 years, today referred to by Icelanders as the 'golden age', saw a blossoming of culture on the Iceland. Most of the events during the period of settlement were recorded in the sagas, Iceland's national cultural treasures. Many Icelanders are proud to point out that they are able to read the medieval texts in the original.

Dark times set in after 1262. At first, Iceland was under Norwegian rule and then fell to the Danish crown. Free trade was limited; self-determination on a national level or in legal matters was a thing of the past; a host of natural disasters laid waste to the land and killed man and beast alike. Famine, epidemics and extreme poverty, as described by Iceland's literature Nobel laureate Halldór Laxness in his novel Iceland's

mark confiscates church property

1602–1854
Danish trade monopoly leads to the economic impoverishment of Iceland

1874
The new constitution grants the Althing legislative power and control of all financial affairs

1904
Hannes Hafsteinn succeeds the Danish governor as the first Icelandic Prime Minister

1944
Declaration of the Republic of Iceland in Þingvellir

Bell, were the result. Cultural life came to a standstill. For a long time, this era cast a shadow over relations between the Icelanders and the Danes, whom they experienced as colonial masters. However, after a struggle lasting almost 100 years, independence was achieved – finally – in 1944.

While the other European countries suffered during World War II and its aftermath, Iceland profited from it in many ways. The American occupation in particular enabled a rapid expansion of infrastructure on the Iceland in the 1940s. The Ring Road and the international airport were built, and Reykjavík grew, since workers were needed to carry out these projects. In addition, a shift had taken place over the previous decades from agriculture to fishing which also boosted the wealth of towns and villages. The relationship between Americans and Icelanders was strained when Keflavík was designated as a base for American troops in 1946. Fear of a return to colonial rule was great, yet at the same time the Americans opened the door for Iceland to the modern era through music, cars and an attitude towards life to match. Some believe that the Icelanders were virtually catapulted from the Middle Ages into the 20th century as a result.

> **Iceland profited from World War II**

Iceland is a modern country, and some past visitors may have been a little disappointed to find that its people no longer live in little turf houses, but in high-rise blocks built to withstand earthquakes. These days, architects often use Icelandic materials, as can be seen especially at the Blue Lagoon; the service building and the hotel with its famous lake are clad in lava bricks and set amidst a landscape of lava.

For many years, Iceland was considered to be a veritable paradise thanks to its steadily growing economy. The year 2008, however, showed that this prosperity was merely on loan, so to speak. After years of full employment, unemployment reared its ugly head again, and inflation reached double figures for a time. In 2011, it looked like the country was back on track and the ever-popular tunnel projects were poised to get under way once more. Aside from the fishing industry, Iceland clung on to the – not uncontroversial – practice of aluminium production, and tourism is as important an economic factor as ever.

1952–75
«Cod wars»: international disputes over national fishing limits which the Icelanders extend to 200 miles

1993 / 2001
Entry into the European Economic Area (EEA) and signing of the Schengen Agreement

2008
A financial and banking crisis brings the country to the brink of bankruptcy

2010
The volcano Eyjafjallajökull erupts. The clouds of ash it produces paralyse European air travel for many days

Superb views open up over the glacial landscapes of Vatnajökull

Iceland welcomes visitors all year round. In summer, three months of daylight are the attraction, during which hardly anyone seems to sleep, and many work outside until midnight. In this time, the flora truly bursts into life, and even on the wide highland plateaux cushions of brilliant pink moss campion carpet the ground. The midnight sun, low in the sky, transforms the landscape into an enchanted golden realm and paints the glacier-topped mountains in glowing deep red

Dancing Northern Lights – magical, mythical and bewitching

and violet hues. In September and early October, autumnal colours dominate, and the hillsides and plains resemble many-coloured patchwork blankets. During the long winter nights, you can marvel at the fascinating spectacle of the dancing, vibrating Northern Lights – magical, mystical and bewitching.

Iceland is by no means a land of silence – in many places, you are distinctly aware of hearing nothing but the sound of nature: the rush of the waves over pebble beaches; the thundering waterfalls; the chorus of birdsong. The first great Icelandic composer of the 20th century, Jón Leifs, was inspired by these sounds, leading him to compose such impressive works as Geysir and Hekla. Art, too, is much influenced by Iceland's natural landscape and history, as Reykjavík's museums clearly demonstrate. The young and dynamic cultural scene has made a name for itself on an international level, and the country has brought forth many multi-talented artists. Some are successful not only as authors, but also as painters; another is one of the founders of the band Sugarcubes and today writes children's opera. Ultimately, though, it is nature which overwhelms you in a way which has captivated so many travellers in the past and which makes you want to come back again and again.

WHAT'S HOT

1 Restaurant goes clubbing

All change In the daytime, the in-vogue *Café Oliver* dishes out Indian food; at the weekend, the place resounds to DJ beats *(Laugavegur 20a, Reykjavík; photo)*. It's mostly students who love *Kaffi Sólon*. The sound of daytime chat gives way to cocktails and loud music in the evenings *(Bankastræti 7a, Reykjavík)*. Other locations which blend day into night, *Hverfisbarinn (Hverfisgata 20, Reykjavík)* and the cosy *Prikid (Bankastræti 12, Reykjavík)*, appeal to the same clientele.

All about fish

2

Off-beat This everyday ingredient is transformed into something very special in Reykjavík. The fishing nation can't do without this staple, but a little variety on the plate is called for. At the *Fish Market (Aðalstræti 12)*, everything revolves around the scaly sea dweller: how about teriyaki trout or monkfish with goat's cheese and coriander? The *Square* also devotes its attention to this typical product of Icelandic kitchens, but with a twist; the watchword here is molecular gastronomy *(Hafnarstræti 20; photo)*. The *VOX Restaurant* abides by its principles, but its New Nordic Cuisine gives a new take on fish *(Suðurlandsbraut 2)*.

3 Creative gear

Import-Export Cool clothes don't just come from abroad. Icelanders are creative and fashion conscious, as the label *Forynja* shows. Styles are colourful and exuberant – perfect for a night on the town *(Laugavegur 12, Reykjavík; www.forynja.is)*. The designs at *Figura* also have a decidedly tongue-in-cheek look to them. Prints are a speciality; not just T-shirts, but also cool whale-shaped cushions or sweet vintage dresses *(Skólavörðustígur 22, Reykjavík)*.

Vatnavinir project

Turn it on The Blue Lagoon, just outside the capital, is a household name, but there are other hot springs worth visiting scattered across the country. The not-for-profit organisation *Vatnavinir* is committed to making springs accessible so that they can be used sustainably *(www.vatnavinir.is)*. Among the organisation's 'customers' is the country's oldest hot spring; at a family hotel in Heydalur, the water bubbles out of the ground *(www.farmholidays.is/FarmDetails /190/heydalur; photo)*. In Krossnes, *Vatnavinir* promotes hot pots with a sea view. In the village of Drangsnes, you can hop out of your car into the hot water – where you're likely to find the odd local resident waiting for you *(on the road through Drangsnes; www.drangsnes.is)*.

Size isn't everything

Beer Micro-breweries are mushrooming up all over Iceland. One of the first was *Bruggsmiðjan*, which has progressed from a miniature undertaking to a most successful operation. The dark 'Kaldi Dökkur' comes highly recommended. Fascinating guided tours and tastings are also on offer at the brewery in Árskógssandur (*Öldugatu 22*). If you don't want to travel that far north, visit Stykkishólmur. This is the home of *Mjöður Brugghús (Hamraendar 5)* and with it a whole host of liquid specialities. The hops, incidentally, come from Bavaria, and the quality of German beer is no secret! One of the country's best beers is produced on a tiny farm. The *Ölvisholt* brewery (photo) doesn't have guided tours, but its chocolaty Lava Imperial Stout and Co. are available nationwide from *Vinbudin (www.vinbudin.is)*.

IN A NUTSHELL

AMERICA

Icelanders were the first Europeans to set foot on American soil. After Erik the Red landed on the south coast of Greenland in AD 982, Bjarni Herjólfsson, on a journey to Greenland in 985, was thrown off course westwards and sighted unfamiliar territory. It wasn't until 1000 AD that Leifur Eiríksson set out to discover this land. He put ashore at three locations in what is today Canada and named them Helluland, Markland and Vínland. Some years later, Þorfinnur Karlsefni and his wife Guðríður, tried to establish a settlement in Vínland, but because of conflicts with the indigenous people, returned to Iceland three years later. For the next 350 years, Greenlandic Icelanders especially used to go to Canada for timber. In the mid-13th century, these discoveries were written down in Eiрík's Saga which was later presumably read by Columbus.

ART

Iceland rates not only as a land of literature with a passion for reading — there are some 40 publishing houses serving its 320,000 inhabitants after all. It has long since become an exciting place for music and the creative arts, too. Björk and Sigur Rós are no longer just familiar to insiders on the music scene, and every year music agents travel to the 'Icelandic Airwaves' festival to hear what's making the news. Since 2006, the 'Sequences' art festival has taken place alongside this, giving young artists in

Photo: Bathing in the Blue Lagoon

Power up and wind down: the Icelanders have lived with all manifestations of volcanic activity since time immemorial

particular a platform to show their works. Creative art has always been deeply influenced by nature, often taking it as its theme; in the past as classical landscape painting and today as part of a more critical dialogue.

Iceland's artists are not only creative; they are also politically active. In 2009, author and comedian Jón Gnarr founded *Besti flokurinn* (the Best Party), and, as its leader, entered the race to become Mayor of Reykjavík in 2010. He won outright, taking 34 per cent of the vote. For the first time, figures other than the familiar faces in politics were starting to take on new roles. Against a backdrop of political corruption, Jón Gnarr is working with 'untainted' artists in a coalition with the Social Democrats.

BATHING

Every town or village, no matter how small, has an open-air swimming pool, as swimming is a compulsory subject at schools and not only keeps you fit, but is also good for your communication skills! Communal bathing in the pleasantly warm *hot pots* brings together politicians and managers, sportsmen and poets; this is the place to exchange news and views. Politician and poet Snorri Sturluson (1179–1241) was an early fan of such consultations in his bathtub 'Snorra-laug' in Reykholt, which he had specially built for the purpose. Icelanders enjoy this outdoor pastime all year round, irrespective of wind and weather. It's a big hit in snowfall!

ENERGY & INDUSTRY

Thanks to the presence of volcanoes and enormous quantities of water, the Icelanders can meet over 90 per cent of their energy needs with these natural resources. They only require oil for transport purposes. Geothermal energy is used in the form of superheated steam or hot water. Almost 90 per cent of households are heated in this way, as are over 200,000m²/0.07mi² of greenhouse space. The other main source of energy is hydroelectric power. It currently only accounts for around 20 per cent, although Icelanders have the highest per capita electricity consumption in the world. The total energy potential of hydroelectric power is estimated to be 220 terawatt hours per year, and the people here are keen to use it, especially for the expansion of aluminium production. Plans for additional aluminium-smelting plants have been in existence for some time, but the economic crisis of 2008 saw virtually all building projects on the island put on hold. Today the three current smelting plants still manage to produce enough aluminium to generate exports of over 30 per cent. Construction of a new smelter on the Reykjanes Peninsula was begun in 2010.

Even though Icelandic electricity counts as regenerative energy, there is valid criticism in the country of the planned aluminium-smelting plants. Firstly, new power plants have to be built to supply such facilities, which interferes consider-

The trademark Icelandic horses are known the world overferde

ably with the natural environment. Secondly, residents, now acutely aware of the financial aspects of the matter since the crisis, are not being comprehensively informed about the costs involved and any price agreements made with smelting-plant operators.

A far better idea is to use the existing energy to heat more greenhouses. Since the financial meltdown, there has been a drive on Iceland to produce more tomatoes, lettuces, paprika, etc. Outside greenhouses, too, you can see cautious attempts at cultivating arable crops and, of course, potatoes.

FAUNA

The arctic fox is the only land mammal which was native to Iceland before human settlement; the rest were brought to the island by man. In summer you can observe herds of sheep wandering across the countryside, even in the most faraway corners. Sheep numbers have been reduced over the last 20 years by 300,000 to 450,000 – firstly, because they destroy the precious layer of vegetation, and secondly, overproduction had to be cut back. The Icelandic horses are renowned the world over; a small breed, superbly adapted to the varied terrain and one which even inexperienced riders can venture out on. What's more, the East of the island is home to around 3000 wild reindeer whose ancestors were imported from Norway in the 18th century.

Alongside the many and varied fish species, the seas around Iceland are populated by numerous marine mammals. Minke whales and orcas (killer whales) can be spotted on whale-watching excursions, as can porpoises. On the coasts, you will often come across various species of seal which also breed here.

First and foremost, however, Iceland is a paradise for birds. Tens of thousands of seabirds nest on the steep rocky cliffs: black guillemot, razorbill, fulmar, gannet, guillemot and puffin. Inland there are huge colonies of pink-footed goose, and rare species of European duck, such as the harlequin and long-tailed varieties, splash about on Lake Mývatn. Often you can see the large bluish-black raven and from time to time a white-tailed sea eagle or even a gyrfalcon.

FISHING INDUSTRY

Around 37 per cent of Icelandic exports are marine produce, caught in the 'fresh and clean waters of the North Atlantic', as claimed by the advertising gurus. Due to the 200-mile fishing zone – a hard-fought result of the so-called 'cod wars' waged primarily against Great Britain – the area which can be exploited economically around Iceland measures some 758,000km^2/0.3mi^2. To preserve stocks of the most important species fished – cod, haddock, redfish, saithe and capelin – annual quotas are laid down. High-tech processing plants operate with flexible production systems so they can react quickly to market demands. The most important processing forms are salting, deep-freezing and drying. Many trawlers have processing facilities on board, a fact which led in the 1990s to the ruin of many smaller fish factories. The main export regions are the USA, Japan and Europe.

FLORA

When the first settlers arrived in the 9th century, Iceland was cloaked in dense birch woods, and vegetation covered 40 per cent of the landscape. Overgrazing, deforestation and subsequent erosion destroyed the top layer of soil; numerous volcano eruptions were another destructive factor. It took a re-forestation and re-cultivation plan to turn 23 per cent of the island into cultivatable land again. Almost 65 per cent, however, is still wasteland.

Vegetation consists of bushy shrubs and trees, such as the northern birch or the willow. Colourful meadows full of a variety of herbaceous plants, such as the purple cranesbill, thrive on the mountain slopes. On the barren plains you'll find varieties of saxifrage, for example, the pink moss campion, and along river banks the glowing purple blossoms of the arctic fireweed and carpets of green moss. Berries, fungi and brown-grey-green lichen *fjallagras* enrich the Icelandic menu.

GEYSERS

The Great Geysir in Haukadalur was mentioned as early as 1294, and Bishop Brynjólfur Sveinsson described it for the first time using the word 'geysir' (geyser in English), thus establishing the designation for all such hot-water spouts. Chemist Robert Bunsen studied the workings of this phenomenon on a trip to Iceland in 1846. He discovered that the water temperature increased, the further down in the geyser column he took his measurements. His explanation was that as the water depth increases, pressure rises and with it the boiling point. The pressure of the steam generated underground must consequently build up to such an extent that it is stronger than the pressure of the water above it in the 5m/16.5ft-deep column. The steam then forces the water upwards, causing the familiar jet of water to erupt.

NAMES

Names in Iceland – nothing could be simpler! First comes the first name, followed by the father's name with the suffix *-son* (son) or *-dóttir* (daughter). The names in a typical family could look something like this: father Einar Jóhannson and mother Svava Elíasdóttir have a son, Gísli Einarsson, and a daughter, Jórunn Einarsdóttir. As you can see, there is no common family name, only patronyms, father's names. People address each other by their first name, under which they are also to be found in the telephone book.

SAGAS

These usually opulent works originated in the 13th century and relate

WHALING

Iceland's stance on whaling has hit the headlines in the American and European media on a number of occasions in recent years. In 2003, under the guise of a scientific programme, whaling was resumed with a catch of around 50 minke whales. Since 2006, the fisheries ministry has allowed commercial whaling once again – the quota lies at a total of 190 animals, and the hunting of fin whales is permitted. One of the most important arguments in favour of the re-commencement of whaling was, and still is, that these giant mammals eat up too much of the prey which commercially fished species rely on to survive; they are in competition with human fishermen. Alongside Norway and Japan, Iceland is one of the few nations to still practise commercial whaling.

above all to the clans around the time of the settlement of Iceland. Family feuds, revenge, betrayal, murder, even love are the main themes – in short, the classic stuff of literature. The sagas are Iceland's cultural treasures, and to this day their heroes, such as Gunnar, wise Njáll or Grettir the Strong, are well known and loved. This is Iceland's very own brand of medieval literature. One of the most significant authors was Snorri Sturluson. He composed the Edda named after him, the Snorra Edda (Prose Edda), written to familiarize the skalds (court poets) of the day with metrics and rhyme. The verses tell of the gods and heroes of prehistoric times, the origins of the world and its ultimate destruction, *Ragnarök*.

VOLCANIC ACTIVITY

With its 15–20 million years, Iceland is one of the youngest regions of the world from a geological point of view – and is still evolving. Volcanic activity, seething thermal zones, the movement of the glaciers and the constant drifting apart of two major continental plates are changing Iceland's landscape all the time. The active volcanic belt traverses the country from Reykjanes in the southwest to Öxarfjörður in the northeast. Two further such areas are on the Snæfellsnes peninsula and in the south.

For geologists, Iceland is like an illustrated textbook, featuring many types of volcano and rock formations – such as ropy lava or obsidian – thermal areas, solfataras (sulphur vents) and geysers.

Most of the 30 or more volcanic systems in these areas have a central volcano or a mountain range with a caldera (a large, round crevasse such as at Askja). Since the settlement of the island, around 250 eruptions, some of them lasting months or years, have taken place in 15 volcanic systems. Some 45,000m³/1588,875ft³ of

rock has been created in the process. The most active central volcanoes are Hekla, Katla and Grímsvötn, each one clocking up over 20 eruptions. In recent years, there have been several such events which not only caused damage for the farmers in southern Iceland, but which also saw international air travel brought to a standstill for days on end. In Iceland's 'Hell's kitchen', things are constantly on the boil.

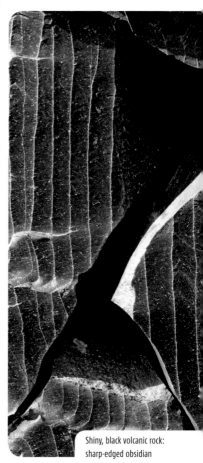

Shiny, black volcanic rock: sharp-edged obsidian

FOOD & DRINK

Traditionally, Icelandic cooking is simple and down-to-earth: fish, meat, potatoes, cereals and milk products. Various techniques have been used – and still are – to preserve fish and meat, including souring, smoking, drying, curing or pickling in whey.

Some old recipes have lived on into the present day and are eaten particularly at the winter feast *Þorrablót*. For the Icelanders this is a way of driving out the winter. Eating foods preserved in the traditional manner harks back to earlier centuries and symbolises the return of fresh foods to the table.

Only when greenhouses were constructed did local production of tomatoes, cucumbers, paprika, lettuce and mushrooms begin. Until then, only rhubarb and cabbage had been grown. Some supermarkets have an impressive stock of fresh vegetables and fruit, imported from all over the world. In recent years, the Icelanders have enriched their diet – largely consisting of meat and fish – by the addition of ‚greens' which were previously frowned upon. This variety is also reflected in the range of places to eat – from Asian restaurants through fast-food chains to rustic Viking pubs, you'll find just about everything.

Due to the economic crisis, the selection of foodstuffs available has changed, and so, too, have eating habits. The trend towards emphasising regional specialities has also hit Iceland. People are reviving old recipes or experimenting with them, for example, horsemeat is some-

Photo: Terrace of the Café Paris in Reykjavík

Fish, fish and more fish: from dried fish to wild salmon – Iceland's chefs are dab hands with the sea's harvest

times used instead of lamb for smoked *hangikjöt*. The vegetables on offer are coming increasingly from Icelandic greenhouses, since imports are still very expensive as a result of the collapse of the currency. Even native cereals are being cultivated, a fact made possible due to climatic change and the creation of resistant types of grain. For the consumer, this is definitely an advantage. Holiday-makers should make a point of looking for typical restaurants and foods in the different regions.

Where both fish and meat are concerned, quality is a top priority, and all products are home-produced. Almost everything from the rivers and the sea lands on a plate in some form or other. Apart from the usual sources of meat, foal is also on the menu, and, in the poultry department, *svartfugl* (razorbill), whose large, colourful eggs also appear on the shelves in spring. Some supermarkets have fresh meat and fish counters, otherwise pre-packed products are to be found on re-frigerated shelves. There are a number of

LOCAL SPECIALITIES

▶ **blóðmór** – Sheep's blood sausage, boiled and eaten with *lifrarpylsa*
▶ **brennivín** – Icelandic aquavit nicknamed the 'black death' because of its label (and knock-out quality!)
▶ **hákarl** – Greenland shark, fermented in open wooden crates and then dried over several months. When washed down with a slug of *brennivín*, palatable even for non-Icelanders (photo, left)
▶ **hangikjöt** – Smoked lamb. Cooked with potatoes, béchamel sauce and peas, it is a traditional Christmas dish. Sliced and eaten cold on rye pancakes (*flatkökur*)
▶ **harðfiskur** – Dried fish. Haddock, cod or catfish dried in the open air and served as a snack with butter (photo, right)
▶ **lifrarpylsa** – Liver sausage made from lamb's liver. Together with *blóðmór*, one of the family of sheep's sausages known as *slátur*
▶ **mýsa** – Whey which has separated from skyr. A refreshing drink

▶ **plokkfiskur** – Stew consisting of potatoes, fish and onions
▶ **rúgbrauð** – Dark, sweet bread, in some places baked in the hot springs
▶ **saltkjöt** – Salted lamb, boiled and eaten cold
▶ **skyr** – Cream cheese made from skimmed milk. Popular dessert with milk or cream and brown sugar
▶ **svið** – Singed sheep's head. The cleaned heads are boiled in saltwater and served with mashed potatoes or swede. Eaten cold as a starter or as a packed lunch for on the road
▶ **sviðasulta** – Brawn made of sheep's head in aspic
▶ **vatn** – Water, direct from the spring or the tap – always enjoyable
▶ **ýmis súrmatur** – Various soured meats, such as blood sausage, liver sausage and boiled ram's testicles which have been marinated in *mýsa* (whey) for 3–4 months

small fishmonger's shops in Reykjavík which sell auk and their eggs when in season. In some places, you can buy freshly caught fish from the fishermen as they come in to harbour.

Icelanders love eating – and in great quantities; individual meals are correspondingly lavish. A decent breakfast buffet includes cornflakes with *súrmjólk* (soured milk) and brown sugar, bread, a selection of cold meats, jam – made, for example, from home-grown berries – tomatoes, cucumber and of course *síld* (herring), marinated in a variety of sauces.

Lunchtime is usually from noon to 1pm, and most of the working population are out to lunch at this time. Restaurants put on appropriate menus, consisting of soup and a fish dish for a reasonable price of around 15 euros. Among the more popular choices are *ýsa* (haddock), *þorskur* (cod) and *karfi* (redfish), either steamed or grilled.

In the afternoon, you'll find a range of cakes, catering to both sweet and savoury tastes. The impressive-looking creamy gateaux are loaded with calories, whereas the *pönnukökur* (crêpes), filled with cream or jam, and *kleinur* (doughnuts) are a little lighter. *Flatbrauð* is a pancake made out of rye flour and is topped with a thin slice of *hangikjöt* (smoked lamb). Sandwiches with *rækja* (shrimps) and mayonnaise are also popular afternoon snacks.

Evening meals are mostly eaten at home and are the most important of the day. At the weekend, many Icelanders like to round off the week with a visit to a restaurant. A number of the internationally trained chefs create highly imaginative dishes from local produce, often inspired by Asian or Mediterranean cuisine. The salmon is excellent, whether smoked or grilled. Farmed salmon is available all year round, and in summer the wild variety is fished from the salmon rivers for which Iceland is famous. *Reyktur silungur* INSIDER TIP (smoked trout) is a speciality of the region around Mývatn and tastes particularly tangy as it is smoked over juniper wood. Should you choose *lamb* as your main course, you'll have to pay considerably more than for fish (around 30 euros), but it's worth it. The lambs

roam freely across the meadows in summer, eating only grasses and herbs, which is why their meat has a slightly ,seasoned' flavour. Another speciality is *hreindýr* (reindeer) – for venison experts a real treat. You'll often come across restaurants advertising *hvalur* (whale meat). This is fried like a steak and, as

Beer has now replaced the traditional mead

befits an animal of this size, has a pretty overwhelming taste. Due to its relatively low price, whale meat was once a typical staple of poor fishing families.

A sumptuous evening meal should be accompanied by wine; tap water is served with all meals. It is of such high quality that it is even exported. This is also the reason why Icelandic beer tastes so good. The trademark beverage, however, is coffee. It is the essential conclusion to every meal and a permanent feature of every get-together. In the evening, Icelanders like to pep it up with cognac or a liqueur. Coffee is relatively cheap, especially when you consider that the second cup usually comes free.

SHOPPING

So you might not be able to take the volcanoes with you, but a candlestick or salt cellar made of lava is a realistic alternative. The area of design in particular has plenty on offer – sometimes kitschy, sometimes creative, but always typically Icelandic. You'll find the appropriate outlets on a stroll through the shopping malls *Kringlan (Reykjavík)* and *Smáralind (Kópavogur)*; otherwise it's worth a foray into streets such as Laugavegur in Reykjavík city centre.

COSMETICS

A cosmetics range going under the label *Blue Lagoon* has been manufactured, based on the special minerals present in the lagoon of the same name. Apart from at the spa itself, the products are also available in tourist areas as well as in the cosmetics departments of the shopping malls. At the *Nature Baths* at Mývatn *(see p. 65)* they also sell their own skin care range, which so far is only available here.

FASHION DESIGN

Since Icelanders have long been very fashion-conscious, you can buy all big-name labels here. Icelandic designer brands, however, are something special. *ELM* uses only alpaca wool and pima cotton to make its elegant outfits. If you like things a touch more extravagant, head for INSIDER TIP *Spaksmannsspjarir* for fashions inspired by the Icelandic landscape *(www.spaksmannsspjarir.is)*. Designs by *GuSt* are characterised by classic details; the designer also incorporates Icelandic wool and fish skin into her creations. Unusual items made from surprising materials are to be had at INSIDER TIP *Kirsuberjatréð* in Reykjavík's Vesturgata: fish-skin bags, jewellery made from bits of plastic hosepipe or felt and organza evening dresses *(www.kirs.is)*. The Icelandic label *66° North* manufactures excellent outdoor fleece garments.

JEWELLERY

Icelandic gold- and silversmiths produce small and very fine individual pieces, some inspired by the Viking era, others incorporating the island's semi-precious gemstones and each with its own particular style. The prize-winning jewellery designed by *Dýrfinna Torfadóttir* is highly unconventional. You can buy it at a number of places, including in Reykjavík at *Mona (Laugavegur 66)*, in Ísafjörður *(Gullauga)* and Akranes

Wool, fashion and cosmetics: Icelandic designers give typical native materials an off-beat twist

(Laugarbraut 15 | tel. 4564660), which is also the site of her atelier.

LAMB & SALMON

If Icelandic cooking is to your taste, you might like to try out some recipes at home using original Icelandic lamb. Delicious vacuum-packed lamb chops are easy to transport. You can find them in every supermarket, as well as at cooperatives such as in Hvammstangi in the North. Round off your menu with a few slices of salmon. By the way, at the *Icemarket* at the airport, you'll find a large selection of Icelandic foods.

SOUND & VISION

A beautiful coffee-table book by an Icelandic photographer is an ideal souvenir. But let's not forget music, either; you'll find a fine selection of CDs and help on hand to guide you through it in Reykjavík at *12 Tónar (Skólavörðustigur 15)*.

WOOL

The classic souvenir from Iceland is of course the Iceland pullover. Wool from Icelandic sheep has superb properties: the long top layer of wool is water-repellent and the finer fibres underneath are as soft and light as mohair. On offer are a range of items, from clothing to cosy blankets.

Apart from tourist shops, which also offer top-quality products, there are cooperatives and individual knitters and weavers in the countryside who sell their wares direct. Nowadays, more fashionable designs are available, alongside the traditional patterns. You'll find the biggest selection in and around Reykjavík, for example at *Iceland Wool (Þingholtsstræti 20 | tel. 5622116)* and at *Rammagerðin (Hafnarstræti 19 | tel. 5517760)*. ● Beautiful, hand-knitted models – what else? – can be found at *Víkurprjón* in Vík í Mýrdal *(Austurvegur 20 | tel. 4871250)*.

THE PERFECT ROUTE

IN THE HOT POT & TO THE WATERFALL

Take the plunge into the waters of the ❶ *Blue Lagoon* → p. 39 and recover from your flight. Via Grindavík you now follow the mountain road (Rte. 427) leading along the coast as far as Rte. 38 which takes you to Hveragerði. Neighbouring ❷ *Selfoss* → p. 48 is an ideal starting point for short trips in the vicinity, e.g. to Gullfoss and Geysir. At the same time, you can get to know a typical, small Icelandic town. The Ring Road (Rte. 1) takes you on eastwards to Hvolsvöllur, where you can find out about the Njál's Saga, past ❸ *Skógafoss* → p. 51 (photo, left) and the first glaciers.

BEACHES, WOODS & GLACIERS

Near Vík, below the glacier ❹ *Mýrdalsjökull* → p. 50, lies what is probably Iceland's prettiest beach – worth a walk in any weather. Then drive across the wide sandar plain, which is either blue or green, depending on the season, on account of the masses of lupins growing there. At the foot of Iceland's largest glacier, Vatnajökull, immerse yourself in the world of ❺ *Skaftafell* → p. 59 with its glacier snouts and woodlands. On ❻ *Jökulsárlón* → p. 59 you'll see drifting blue and black icebergs, which you can marvel at over coffee and cake at the restaurant Jökulsárlón. The rest of the route is a real showstopper, thanks to the nearby glacier and the captivating sight of its ice sparkling in the sunlight.

FJORDS & SEABIRDS

From ❼ *Höfn* → p. 57 the route takes you into the uplands, that is, on the coast road along the eastern fjords. These are dotted with charming little villages such as ❽ *Djúpivogur* → p. 53, a fantastic place for a spot of bird-watching. Follow the coastline along Rte. 96 which later joins Rte. 92. A detour to Reyðarfjörður lets you take a look at one of Iceland's largest industrial sites.

LAKES, VOLCANOES & WHALES

From ❾ *Egilsstaðir* → p. 54 there are opportunities to head off for the highlands and the Hálslón reservoir or to the picturesque harbour of Seyðisfjörður. The next stage of the journey to the lake, ❿ *Mývatn* → p. 64, skirts the edge of the highlands – time and again you will be rewarded with thrilling views of this extraor-

Experience the many facets of Iceland on a round trip taking in geysers, harbours and lakes

dinary landscape, shaped by volcanic eruptions. A bus trip into the highlands to the ⑪ *Askja* → p.81 is a further highlight. Whale fans should make a detour to ⑫ *Húsavík* → p. 65 for a visit to the Whale Museum.

CITY STROLL & HISTORY LESSON

After these imposing natural spectacles, it's off to the jewel in the North's crown, ⑬ *Akureyri* → p. 60, to immerse yourself in 'city' life once more. The journey through the mountains is followed by the opening up of a gently undulating landscape around ⑭ *Varmahlíð* → p.66, green and, above all, agricultural in character. The region boasts several historically significant sites, for example, the former bishop's seat of ⑮ *Hólar* → p. 67.

ON THE WATER & TO THE CAPITAL

Now, continue southwest, and take the chance to visit the ⑯ *Snæfellsnes Peninsula* → p. 68 (photo, right), combined with a boat excursion from Stykkishólmur or even a foray onto the glacier. First of all, you follow Rte. 59, then Rte. 60 and Rte. 54 which bring you to ⑰ *Borgarnes* → p. 68. Here, you can find out more about another literary gem, Egil's Saga, and set out for historic ⑱ *Reykholt* → p. 71. From Borgarnes, either drive through the tunnel or take the prettier option of Rte. 47 along the Hvalfjörður to ⑲ *Reykjavík* → p. 32.

1900km/1180mi. Driving time: 38 hours.
Recommended trip length: 10–14 days.
Detailed map of the route on the back cover, in the road atlas and the pull-out map.

REYKJAVÍK

MAP INSIDE THE BACK COVER

Reykjavík (119 D5) (*M E9*) is a modern, dynamic city and growing fast. You'll get probably the best view over Reykjavík (119,000 inh.) and the surrounding area from the tower of the Hallgrímskirkja or from Perlan, taking in the colourful city-centre houses, the smart neighbourhood of villas and gardens, the domestic airport and the new apartment blocks: urban life, fenced in by the sea and the Esja peak.

In 1786, Reykjavík, together with four other Icelandic towns, was granted municipal status. At that time, only 170 people lived there; today, 65 per cent of the Iceland population live in Greater Reykjavík, to which the towns of Kópavogur and Hafnarfjörður also belong. This process of continual development began with the expansion of the fishing industry at the beginning of the 20th century, as Reykjavík has a favourably situated harbour. After 1940, the occupying English and American forces began to build up infrastructure, thereby generating employment.

Reykjavík is a young city, a fact which is physically demonstrated by the architecture – only a few buildings date back to the 19th century. It's young at heart, too, being the location of the university and numerous schools; children and young people throng the streets and squares. In summer, especially, when everyone is trying to soak up as much sun as possible, the street cafés and green open spaces are packed with people.

Photo: The 'Sun-Craft' sculpture at Reykjavík harbour

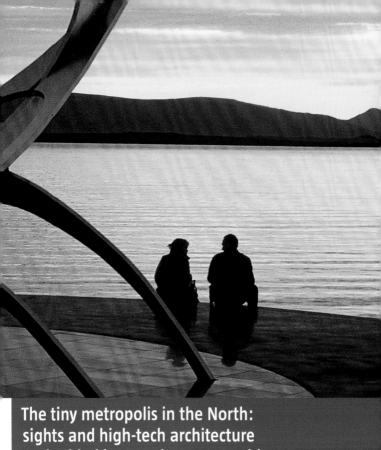

The tiny metropolis in the North: sights and high-tech architecture embedded in stunning countryside

CITY **WHERE TO START?**

The tourist centre is the old part of the city between the Tjörnin lake and the harbour. Central bus station: Lækjartorg. City Hall, with an underground car park, is located here, as is **Austurvöllur (U B3)** *(⑪ b3)* square and the Parliament building, Hotel Borg, Dómkirkja and cafés. From here, head for the Harbour House and the shopping street, Laugavegur.

Reykjavík is not only the economic and political heart of the country, but also its cultural capital. In 2011, Unesco named Reykjavík a 'City of Literature', the fifth to bear the title. Many galleries, which give young, lesser known artists a platform for their work, can be found in the little side streets off the main thoroughfare *Laugavegur.* In Reykjavík's quirky designer shops and its lively cafés and bars, there's a discovery waiting to be made around every corner.

The 76m/250ft-high Hallgrímskirkja with the monument to Leifur Eiríksson

SIGHTSEEING

AÐALSTRÆTI (U B3) (*m b3*)
Probably Reykjavík's oldest street. At its southern end, excavation work brought to light the foundations of a Nordic longhouse from the 10th century which can now be viewed at *Reykjavík 871 +/-2*, a museum focusing on the settlement of the city *(daily 10am–5pm | Admission: 1000 ISK | www.reykjavik871.is)*.

House no. 10 is the oldest house in the city and, in the 18th century, was the location of Iceland's first wool factory. Today, it is the headquarters of the *Handverk & Hönnun* (Crafts & Design) association. At the adjacent INSIDERTIP *Kraum design store* you can buy lots of their highly original products, from items of clothing to everyday objects.

At the end of the street stands an 18th-century *warehouse* from which a tunnel once led to the harbour. It was largely used to smuggle the gyr falcons, kept in cages in the warehouse, to the ships waiting in the harbour to take them to their aristocratic European buyers.

ÁRBÆJARSAFN (0) (*m 0*)
Open-air museum featuring 27 historic buildings, mostly from Reykjavík, dating back to the period from 1820 to 1907. Also special exhibitions, a shop and restaurant. *June–Aug daily 10am–5pm | Admission: 1000 ISK | Kistuhylur 4 | www.arbaejarsafn.is*

ÁSMUNDUR SVEINSSON SCULPTURE MUSEUM (U F4) (*m f4*)
Ásmundur Sveinsson (1893–1982) was one of the country's foremost sculptors. Many of his works are to be seen in Reykjavík, in particular here at the Asmundarsafn. The studio was built in 1942 to his own plans. *May–Sept daily 10am–4pm, Oct–April Sat/Sun 1pm–5pm | Admission: 1000 ISK | Sigtún | www.artmuseum.is*

AUSTURVÖLLUR ★ (U B3) (🗺 b3)

In the centre of this busy square, scene of all political rallies, is the *statue of Iceland's national hero Jón Sigurðsson*, crafted by Einar Jónsson. He looks towards a grey basalt building: the seat of the Icelandic Parliament, the *Alþingishús*. It was built in 1881 and an extension was added in 2001. To the left of this stands Reykjavík's oldest church, *Dómkirkja*, from the year 1776. The eastern side of the square is dominated by the venerable *Hótel Borg*, founded in 1930.

EINAR JÓNSSON MUSEUM ●
(U C4) (🗺 c4)

Einar Jónsson (1874–1954) was the first Icelandic sculptor to champion the symbolist style. A good number of his works stand in Reykjavík, most of these in the sculpture garden adjacent to the museum. *June–15 Sept Tue–Sun 2pm–5pm, 16 Sept–Nov and Feb–May Sat/Sun 2pm–5pm | Admission: 600 ISK | Njarðargata | www.skulptur.is*

HAFNARHÚS (HARBOUR HOUSE) ★
(U B3) (🗺 b3)

The former warehouse on the harbour is the setting for some fantastic exhibition rooms. Focal point of the collection is the work of Icelandic artist Erró, famous for his large-scale paintings which borrow heavily from the comic genre. *Daily 10am–5pm (Thu until 8pm) | Admission: 1000 ISK | Tryggvagata | www.artmuseum.is*

HALLGRÍMSKIRKJA ★ (U C4) (🗺 c4)

You can spot the 76m/250ft-high 🌿 tower of this church from far away; it was named after the pastor and author of the Passion Hymns Hallgrímur Pétursson (1614–74) and is now a famous city landmark. Built to a highly unconventional design by Guðjon Samúelsson, the church can accommodate 1200 worshippers. Pétursson took his inspiration from the verti-

cal arrangement of basalt columns when designing the sweeping tower façade. Construction took over 40 years, and the church was finally consecrated in 1986; the huge organ, built by Klais in Germany, was added in 1992. Regular ● *organ concerts* are staged during the summer months – a real acoustic treat in these bright, generously proportioned surroundings. A *statue of Leifur Eiríksson,* the man who 'discovered' the New World, stands in front of the church. The Stirling Calder sculpture was a gift from the USA in 1930 (to commemorate the 1000th anniversary of the Alþing) and echoes the shape of the tower. *Tower: daily 9am–8pm | Admission: 500 ISK*

HARPA (U C2–3) (🗺 c2–3)

Approaching Reykjavík from the sea, you can't fail to notice the multi-storey, multi-coloured building on the harbour. The Harpa Concert Hall and Conference Centre was officially opened in 2011, following completion of the fascinating glass façade by artist Olafur Elíasson. The building has already bagged its first architecture prize and is set to make a lively contribution to the music scene. Alongside a number of shops, there is also a restaurant and a bar. *Austurbakki 2 | www.harpa.is*

ÞJÓÐMENNINGARHÚS (CULTURE HOUSE) ● (U C3) (🕮 c3)

Venue for changing exhibitions on various aspects of Icelandic culture and history. The collection of medieval manuscripts – recordings of the Eddas and Sagas – is particularly impressive and is Iceland's most important cultural treasure. *Daily 11am–5pm | Admission: 700 ISK, Wed: free | Hverfisgata 15 | www.thjodmenning.is*

LISTASAFN ÍSLANDS (NATIONAL GALLERY) (U B3–4) (🕮 b3–4)

Comprehensive collection of Icelandic art covering the 19th century to the present day and shown in changing exhibitions. Attractive café. *Tue–Sun 11am–5pm | Admission: 800 ISK | Fríkirkjuvegur 7 | www.listasafn.is*

PERLAN ⭐ (U D6) (🕮 d6)

Reykjavík's second show-stopping landmark is a mixture of pragmatism and futurism: the mirrored glass dome mounted on six hot-water tanks known as 'The Pearl', standing on top of a wooded hill, Öskjuhlíð. The interior offers space for receptions and small trade fairs, and one of the tanks houses the Saga Museum. An *artificial geyser* blasts off a jet of water every 15 minutes – comparable to the Strókkur geyser. A ⤋ *viewing platform* has been created on top of the tanks, encircling the dome. From here, you can see

as far as the Snæfellsjökull glacier. Inside, there's a café, but the real highlight is the *gourmet restaurant*, which revolves every two hours. Five minutes from Perlan, there's a second artificial *Geysir* including an explanation of how it works.

PHALLUS.IS (U E4) (🕮 e4)

Penises from all species of mammal – and since 2011 even from a human being – are on display here. The museum also has a number of curiosities and artistic works from around the world. *Daily 11am–6pm | Admission: 1000 ISK | Laugavegur 116 | www.phallus.is*

CITY HALL (U B3) (🕮 b3)

A real architectural eye-catcher, built in 1992 on land specially reclaimed from the Tjörnin. Form and location initially earned much criticism from the population; the building detracted from the pretty row of villas which lined the shore of the inner-city lake. Today, City Hall is a popular venue for receptions and exhibitions in which visitors find themselves almost on a level with the lake's surface. The large 3D representation of Iceland is a 'must-see', too.

FOOD & DRINK

Á NÆSTU GRÖSUM (U C3) (🕮 c3)

Vegetarian restaurant with varying menus and cakes. Very popular. *Laugavegur 20b | tel. 5 52 84 10 | Budget*

BÆJARINS BESTU (U B3) (🕮 b3)

A hit with hot-dog fans; here, you'll find the best-in-class variety – and usually a huge queue of hungry people to match. *Corner of Tryggvagata/Pósthússtræti | Budget*

CAFÉ PARIS (U B3) (🕮 b3)

Complete with a view of the Austurvöllur. In summer, you can sit on the terrace and

Iceland's capital and its gateway on the world: young, dynamic Reykjavík

savour a touch of the Mediterranean. Selection of salads and good cakes. *Austurstræti 14 | tel. 5 51 10 20 | Budget*

ICELANDIC FISH & CHIPS
(U B3) (*𝄞 b3*)

This is the place to mix and match your own version of fish and chips from a range of ingredients – with astonishingly varied results. *Tryggvagata 8 | tel. 5 11 11 18 | Budget*

INSIDER TIP KAFFIVAGNINN
(U B2) (*𝄞 b2*)

Savour the good quality fish dishes at this eatery overlooking the harbour. This is where the fishermen come to eat, too. *Grandagarður 10 | tel. 5 51 59 32 | Budget*

PERLAN ● ☆ (U D6) (*𝄞 d6*)

Fabulous view over Reykjavík and the surrounding area, teamed with much-acclaimed, award-winning cuisine (fish dishes and venison buffet). At the weekend, it's essential to book a table. *Öskjuhlíð 105 | tel. 5 62 02 00 | Expensive*

VEGAMÓT (U C3) (*𝄞 c3*)

A popular place to eat, especially at lunchtime, and for years now one of the places to be in Reykjavík. Big selection of fish dishes and loads of chicken. Eat out on the terrace in summer. *Vegamótastígur 4 | tel. 5 11 30 40 | Moderate*

SHOPPING

The main shopping streets in Reykjavík are *Laugavegur, Hverfisgata* and *Skólavörðurstigur*. In addition to designer stores and fashion boutiques, there are some innovative jeweller's shops. Don't miss the *Eymundsson* bookshop or the CD stores *Skifan* and INSIDER TIP *12tónar*. Here, you'll find the hottest sounds Iceland's music business has to offer.

There are a range of Icelandic and international outlets as well as cafés and cinemas in the ● *Kringlan* and *Smáralind* shopping malls in Kópavogur. At the *Kolaportið flea market* on the harbour, you're bound to discover heaps of stuff you never knew you needed – and probably don't *(Sat/Sun 11am–5pm)!*

SPORTS & ACTIVITIES

● Reykjavík's eight thermal baths have earned it the nickname 'Spa City'. If you just want to relax, head for INSIDER TIP ➤ *Vesturbæjarlaug (Hofsvalla-*

One of Reykjavík's hottest locations: Kaffibarinn

gata (U A3) (*m̂ a3*) | *Admission: 360 ISK).* This is where Reykjavík's movers and shakers hang out. Find out more about the wellness city at *www.spacity.is.*

The route along the coast as far as the bird sanctuary at the ✦ *Grótta light-house* is ideal for an excursion by bike. These can be hired from *Borgarhjól (Hverfisgata 50* (U C3) (*m̂ c3*) | *tel. 5 51 56 53).* Reykjavík is the starting point for any number of different tours and activities, including whale watching. Ask at the tourist information office for details.

BEACH

NAUTHÓLSVÍK (0) (*m̂ 0*)
This popular beach lies on the edge of the Öskjuhlíð recreational area. Thanks to the artificial hot spring, bathers can enjoy a water temperature of 20°C/68°F. *15 May–Aug daily 10am–8pm*

ENTERTAINMENT

BROADWAY (U F4) (*m̂ f4*)
Biggest disco in the city. Varied programme at weekends, with Icelandic and international guests. Dress code: fashionably elegant. *Ármúli 9 | tel. 5 33 11 00 | www.broadway.is*

HÁSKÓLABÍÓ (U A4) (*m̂ a4*)
Cinema at the University. Films are shown in the original language with subtitles. It feels like a cinema, but it's really a lecture theatre. *Hagatorg | tel. 5 30 19 19*

KAFFIBARINN (U C3) (*m̂ c3*)
Cramped, full and trendy. This disco and bar is a 'must-visit' for anyone who has read 101 Reykjavík. *Bergstaðastræti 1*

NASA (U B3) (*m̂ b3*)
Popular disco with broad live-music spectrum. The queues to get in are usually long, though. *Austurvöllur 101 | tel. 5 11 13 13 | Admission: from 1000 ISK*

SINFÓNÍUHLJÓMSVEIT ÍSLANDS (U C2–3) (*m̂ c2–3*)
The Icelandic Symphony Orchestra is highly acclaimed around the world. Concerts often include works by Icelandic composers. *Austurbakki 2 | tel. 5 45 25 00 | www.sinfonia.is*

VOLCANO SHOW (U B4) (*b4*)
Spectacular film showing volcano eruptions in Iceland, including historical footage going back 50 years. Screenings take place all year round with commentaries in English. *Hellusund 6a | tel. 8 45 95 48 | 1 hr: 1200 ISK, 2 hrs: 1500 ISK*

WHERE TO STAY

 # 101 (U D4) (*d4*)
Centrally located guest house. The rooms are modestly equipped and share bathrooms on the corridor. *16 rooms | Laugavegur 101 | tel. 5 62 61 01 | www.iceland101.com | Budget*

BORG (U B3) (*b3*)
Well-established hotel with tasteful, individually furnished rooms and a touch of luxury. *56 rooms | Pósthússtræti 11 | tel. 511 44 0 | www.hotelborg.is | Expensive*

HÓTEL CABIN (U E3) (*e3*)
One of the more reasonably priced hotels in Iceland. The rooms are a little on the small side, but have all the essentials, from minibar to shower. The hotel also has INSIDER TIP rooms without daylight (don't forget, it doesn't get dark here in summer!). *65 rooms | Borgartún 32 | tel. 5 11 60 30 | www.hotelcabin.is | Moderate*

YOUTH HOSTEL (0) (*0*)
Open all year round, the hostel is situated next to the large swimming pool. Bus no. 4 takes you every 20 minutes into the city centre. Accommodation is also available in 8 double rooms. Book in good time, if you're coming in the summer! *164 beds | Sundlaugavegur 34 | tel. 5 53 81 10 | www.hostel.is | Budget*

INSIDER TIP **ROOM WITH A VIEW** ☆
(U C3) (*c3*)
Super-stylish apartments and whirlpools with – not surprisingly – a great view over the city. Ideal for families and for longer stays. *30 apartments | Laugavegur 18 | tel. 5 52 72 62 and 8 69 25 59 | www.roomwithaview.is | Moderate–Expensive*

INFORMATION

TOURIST INFORMATION CENTRE
(U B3) (*b3*)
Aðalstræti 2 | tel. 5 90 15 00 | www.visit reykjavik.is

WHERE TO GO

BESSASTAÐIR (119 D5) (*D–E9*)
The residence of Iceland's president lies on the Álftanes headland and is visible from Reykjavík. The estate belonged to Snorri Sturluson in the 13th century, but fell into Norwegian hands when he was murdered and later still to the Danish crown. The windows of the *church*, which was built between 1780 and 1823, feature motifs from Icelandic history. Near the altar, memorial plaques hang in memory of past presidents. *Irregular opening times*

BLÁA LÓNIÐ (BLUE LAGOON) ★ ●
(118 C6) (*D10*)
The most famous bathing pool in Iceland lies, encircled by a landscape of lava, 40km/25mi to the south-west on the Reykjanes Peninsula. The waters of the milky-blue lake get their colour from the minerals and algae they contain, which also have proven healing properties in the treatment of skin disorders. Depending on the light conditions, the colour changes from turquoise through to deep blue. Bathing in the warm water (38°C/100°F) is relaxing for body and mind, and a peeling with a silica mud mask is a great way to thoroughly cleanse your skin. Other spa offerings include massages and facial treatments. The spa's *restaurant (tel. 4 20 88 06 |*

Moderate–Expensive) serves everything from light dishes to gourmet menus. *June–Aug daily 9am–9pm, Sept–May daily 10am–8pm | Admission: 4500 ISK | www.bluelagoon.com*

HAFNARFJÖRÐUR (119 D5) (*Ø E9–10*)
Fancy meeting a few elves and Vikings? Then Hafnafjörður is the place for you. Situated 12km/7.5mi to the south of Reykjavík, its excellent harbour made it an important trading post and for many centuries the main Hanseatic port on Iceland. To this day, the harbour remains a major commercial centre, not least because of the aluminium smelting plant Straumsvík located close by the town.
Hafnarfjörður was built in the *Búrfellshraun* lava field, which defines the character of the site. It is said that huge elf colonies are hidden in the lava formations, and, following a corresponding plan, you can even take a walk through the imaginary dwellings of the fairy folk *(Tourist Information Office | tel. 5 85 55 00 | www.visithafnarfjordur.is)*. The Vikings, too, felt at home here. Every year, there is a rather over-the-top Viking Festival, organised by the owner of the restaurant *Fjörukráin (Strandgata 55 | tel. 5 65 12 13 | www.vikingvillage.is | Moderate)*. Behind the *Hotel Viking* you'll find INSIDER TIP ▶ The Cave, an imaginatively decorated, themed bar.

VIÐEY (119 D4–5) (*Ø E9*)
Historically and culturally, the little Iceland in the Kollafjörður fjord to the north of the city is a charming place for a day trip. The first settlers were recorded here as early as the 10th century, but the oldest surviving building was constructed on the orders of Skúli Magnússon, the provincial governor, in 1753–55. It is the oldest stone building in the country and is used today as a restaurant *(Budget)*. The tiny church next door dates back to the year 1774.
The signposted footpaths on the Iceland lead you eastwards to the ruins of a village which boasted an international port until the beginning of the 20th century. The last residents moved away in 1943. The west of the Iceland is the setting for Richard Serra's ensemble of standing stones, Afangar, which harmonises perfectly with the landscape and Reykjavík in the background. In 2007, Yoko Ono commissioned the 'Imagine Peace Tower' on Viðey in memory of her husband, John Lennon. *Ferry from Sundahöfn, Skarfabakki | daily 11.15am–5.15pm; every hour from Viðey 11.30am–6.30pm | Admission: 1000 ISK*

ÞINGVELLIR ★ (113 E4) (*Ø F9*)
In terms of the Icelanders' sense of national identity, Þingvellir ('Parliament

Iceland's most important site for over 1100 years now: Þingvellir – National Park and World Heritage Site

Fields') is the most important place in the country. It was designated a National Park back in 1928 and was included in the list of Unesco World Heritage Sites in 2004. This is where all historically significant events in Icelandic history have taken place: from the declaration of the free state in 930 down to the founding of the Republic of Iceland in 1944. The site, 35km/22mi to the east of Reykjavík, was chosen to host the original Althing for its size, reachability for most settlers and the presence of water and grazing areas for their horses. All tribal chiefs, the 'Goden', and free farmers met once a year for 14 days to draw up laws, pass judgement and take political decisions.

From the ☼ observation point, with adjoining *information centre (April–Oct daily 9am–4pm | www.thingvellir.is)*, you have a fine view across the landscape, including Iceland's largest lake, *Þingvallavatn* (85km²/915ft²), the mountains surrounding it and the *Almannagjá* ('Everyman's Ravine'), and the track that runs through it. From the *Lögberg* ('Law

Rock'), the speaker recited the laws; former execution sites are located close by. To the north of the Almannagjá is the *Öxarárfoss* waterfall, which was artificially constructed, presumably in the 10th century, to allow the waters of the Öxará to flow into the plain.

In geological terms, too, Þingvellir is highly significant. It is the continuation of the Mid-Atlantic ridge, where the Eurasian and North-American plates are still drifting apart, as demonstrated by the two ravines, *Almannagjá* and *Hrafnagjá* ('Raven's Ravine') running from the north-east to the south-west. Measurements have shown that Þingvellir is both sinking and widening by 8mm/0.026ft every year.

For divers, **INSIDER TIP** the descent into the *Silfra rift* between the continental plates to a depth of almost 15m/50ft is a memorable experience. There are even night dives on offer *(www.diveiceland. com)*. You'll also find a number of designated campsites in the National Park.

THE SOUTH

The countryside in the South is picture-postcard stuff, with green meadows and pastures and broad, black sandy beaches; further east, these give way to the sandar plains, formed by meltwater deposits, at the foot of the Mýrdalsjökull glacier. Agriculture is the main source of income for the population of southern Iceland.

Since this is one of the most active volcano zones, eruptions are frequent occurrences, Hekla being a regular offender. Eruptions of sub-glacial volcanoes, such as the Eyjafjallajökull in 2010, are particularly dangerous. This one caused not only devastating flooding, but also threw up an ash cloud which brought air traffic in the whole of Europe to a standstill. Farmers in the region were badly affected, as their fields were smothered by a layer of ash. Yet only six months later, little was still to be seen of the ash itself which above all had coloured the glaciers black. Resourceful farmers sold the ash to tourists – a real big seller! In 2011, there were further eruptions; this time it was the Grímsvötn below the Vatnajökull and then in June underneath the Mýrdalsjökull, which in turn triggered a glacier burst destroying part of the Ring Road. The geothermal energy in the South is used to heat the many greenhouses; you can also get an idea of its power at the famous geyser in Haukadalur or at the Hellisheiði power plant.

Only a handful of towns and villages on the south coast have their own harbour; shallow waters and treacherous currents have always made putting into land ex-

Photo: Gullfoss, the 'golden waterfall'

Geysers and legends: Iceland's 'market garden' lies in the flourishing landscape of this active volcanic region

tremely tricky, and fishing boats regularly capsized. Fishing, however, continues to play a key role to this day.

HEIMAEY

(120 A6) (*∅ G12*)★ ● The Vestmannaeyjar Islands ('Westmen Islands') lie to the south-west of Iceland; the southernmost of these, Surtsey, was only formed in 1963–67 and is now a protected area.

The largest and only inhabited island is Heimaey, whose roughly 4100 inhabitants live from fishing and fish processing. The island came to fame on 23 January 1973 when a new volcano erupted. Lava shot out of a 1.6km/1mi-long crevasse, gushing out and smothering the houses and threatening to close the entrance to the harbour. The eruption lasted five months, and the ash buried a third of all buildings. Today, Heimaey is a green town again, whose residents see the lava as a welcome source of building material.

The solidified lava masses at the harbour mouth also provide effective protection against the north-east wind. Since 2005, INSIDER TIP a number of buried houses have been uncovered *(www.pompei ofthenorth.com).*

From Eldfell and the old Helgafell volcano you get a panoramic view of the

SKANSINS

The fortifications above the harbour were constructed by the Danes in the 16th century, but they could not repel the assault by North African pirates in 1627 who carried off half the population into slavery. Parts of their ship's gear can be seen at the Folk Museum. A replica *stave church,*

The puffin, with its multi-coloured bill, is Iceland's unofficial heraldic animal

entire island as far as the south coast of Iceland and the Eyjafjallajökull and Mýrdalsjökull glaciers. Heimaey is an ideal spot for puffin fans – thousands of these seabirds nest in burrows in the slopes of the cliffs around *Herjólfsdalur.*

The 'Herjólfur' ferry plies between Landeyjahöfn and Heimaey several times a day, in stormy weather from Þorlákshöfn. *Tel. 4 81 28 00 | www.eimskip.com | Return ticket: 2000 ISK (from Landeyjahöfn), 5320 ISK (from Þorlákshöfn)*

SIGHTSEEING

BYGGÐASAFN (FOLK MUSEUM)

Everything about the volcano eruptions at Surtsey and Heimaey, including old pictures from the time before 1973. *15 May–15 Sept Mon–Fri 1pm–5pm | Admission: 400 ISK | Ráðhúströð*

a present from Norway to the Icelanders in 2000 on the occasion of the 1000th anniversary of Christianisation, stands alongside the site. Also close by is *Landlyst,* Iceland's first maternity hospital (1847), now a museum *(June–Aug daily 11am–5pm | Admission: 500 ISK).*

SURTSEY (120 A6) *(G12)*

An subsea volcanic eruption formed the island over a period of four years. The process began on 14 November 1963, and the lava flow finally came to a halt on 5 June 1967. Since then, surf and climatic influences have permanently changed the face of the island which is now a strictly protected area and was granted World Heritage Site status by Unesco in 2008. For tourists, boat excursions or sightseeing flights are the only opportunity to take a look at Surtsey.

Information and tours: *Viking Tours (see below)*

CAFÉ MARIA
The café is a favourite meeting place for the island folk, enticed especially by the wide range of eats on offer, from burgers to cod. *Skólavegur 1 | tel. 4 813160 | Budget–Moderate*

FJÓLAN
Large family restaurant. Popular for its fish dishes and the 'Catch of the Day'. *Vestmannabraut 28 | tel. 4 813 663 | Moderate–Expensive*

SPORTS & ACTIVITIES
You can book excursions by boat around the island, including bird- and whale watching trips, at *Viking Tours (Suðurgerði 4 | tel. 4 88 48 84 | www.vikingtours.is)*. Golfers will find a fine 18-hole golf course in *Herjólfsdalur (tel. 4 812 63)*.

ENTERTAINMENT

LUNDINN
There's live music at the weekends down at this pub. *Jun–Aug Fri/Sat 2pm–5am | Kirkjuvegur 21*

WHERE TO STAY

SUNNUHÓLL
Modest rooms, also sleeping-bag accommodation. Breakfast is at the Hotel Þórshamar. *7 rooms | Vestmannabraut 28 | tel. 4 81290 0 | www.hotelvestmannaeyjar.is | Budget*

ÞÓRSHAMAR
Well-equipped rooms, central location, whirlpool and sauna. Staff at the hotel can also help you organise tours of the surrounding region. *21 rooms | Vestmannabraut 28 | tel. 4 8129 00 | www.hotelvestmannaeyjar.is | Moderate*

INFORMATION

TOURIST INFORMATION CENTRE
Located in the Folk Museum. *Ráðhúströð | tel. 4 8135 55 | www.vestmannaeyjar.is*

HVERAGERÐI

(119 E5) (∅ F10) Its sheltered location in a valley and the many thermal springs have earned Hveragerði a reputation as Iceland's 'market garden'.

★ **Heimaey**
The Eldfell volcano ensured the island worldwide fame in the 1970s → p. 43

★ **Hekla**
Once the gateway to Hell and still an active volcano → p. 48

★ **Þórsmörk**
'Thor's Wood' lies protected by glaciers → p. 48

★ **Geysir**
The one that gave its name to all the others → p. 49

★ **Gullfoss**
This waterfall plunges 31m/102ft into the deep → p. 50

★ **Skógar**
An impressive, 60m/197ft-high waterfall and a fine museum → p. 51

MARCO POLO HIGHLIGHTS

Around 60 per cent of all produce grown under glass in the country are cultivated here in over 15ha/0.05mi2 of greenhouses. Since 1939, it has also been the site of the state-run Horticultural College and its experimental gardens and research departments. Alongside vegeta-

FOOD & DRINK

INSIDER TIP ▶ KJÖT & KÚNST

Shop and restaurant selling Icelandic dishes, also vegetarian meals. You can take them away, too. *Breiðamörk 21 | tel. 4 83 50 10 | Budget*

Bananas, palms and geraniums in one of the many greenhouses in Hveragerði

ble growing, tourism is a further important economic factor for the 2300 inhabitants. The town also has a rehabilitation centre for rheumatism sufferers and a sanatorium specialising in naturopathy.

NLFÍ ☺

The cafeteria at the sanatorium offers a wholefood menu. You'll need to book a table, though. *Grænamörk 10 | tel. 4 83 03 00 | Budget*

SIGHTSEEING

THERMAL AREA

One of the town's many thermal areas is situated right in the centre of town. Here you can find out more about the different springs, their uses and geological structure. *May–Aug 8am–6pm | Guided tour including do-it-yourself boiled eggs in the hot spring: 450 ISK | Hveramörk 13 | tel. 4 83 50 62*

SPORTS & ACTIVITIES

You can sign up for riding excursions of various lengths organised by *Elðhestar* (*Vellir | tel. 4 80 48 00 | www.eldhestar.is*).
There are a number of walking tours of the town on offer, as well as more challenging hikes into the thermal areas of the varied countryside of the *Hengill Range*. You can also go for a swim in one of Iceland's oldest and prettiest pools.

Finally, why not relax at the *NLFÍ* sanatorium with an all-over massage and INSIDER TIP> volcanic mud pack *(from 4700 ISK | www.hnlfi.is)?*

WHERE TO STAY

FROST OG FUNI

Stylish rooms, decorated with contemporary art works. Swimming pool, sauna and hot pot on site. *12 rooms | Hverhamar | tel. 4 83 49 59 | www.frostandfire. is | Expensive*

FRUMSKÓGAR

Located in a quite side road. Well-equipped apartments, also with their own *hot pot.* The rooms in the guest house are more modest. *4 rooms, 5 apartments | Frumskógar 3 | tel. 8 96 27 80 | www.frumskogar.is | Budget–Moderate*

INFORMATION

UPPLÝSINGAMIÐSTÖÐ SUÐURLANDS (SOUTH ICELAND INFORMATION)

In the shopping centre. *Sunnumörk 2–4 | tel. 4 83 46 01 | www.southiceland.is*

WHERE TO GO

HELLISHEIÐI (119 E5) (*M F10*)

Just 18km/11mi to the west of Hveragerði is the ● *Hellisheiðarvirkjun* geothermal power plant, situated in a high-temperature zone in the Hengill Range. Steam and hot water are pumped to the surface from a depth of over 2000m/6560ft. The steam is used to generate electricity and the hot water to heat the glacier water. This fresh water is then fed into Reykjavík's district-heating network. Find out more about the technology, current protects and the region as a whole at the plant's visitor centre. *Daily 9am–6pm | tel. 5 16 60 00 | www.or.is*

HVOLSVÖLLUR

(120 A5) (*M G11*) **Commercial centre for the whole region, Hvolsvöllur's 500 inhabitants work largely in the retail and service sectors.**

The region's first cooperative society was founded here in the 1930s, not least because it was a favourable location for farms in the South. Hvolsvöllur is an ideal starting point for tours exploring the origins of Njál's Saga.

SIGHTSEEING

SAGA CENTRE

This is a good place to get a first insight into Njál's Saga and general living conditions in the Middle Ages. Corresponding tours of the area are on offer. Iceland's most popular saga revolves around wise Njál and his friend Gunnar, who fall victim to the thirst for revenge of Gunnar's wife, Hallgerður. *15 May–15 Sept daily 9am–6pm | Admission: 750 ISK | Hlíðarvegur | www.njala.is*

FOOD & DRINK

HLÍÐARENDI

The service station is a popular stopover for travellers, the atmosphere typically Icelandic. *Ring Road | tel. 4 87 81 97 | Budget*

HVOLSVÖLLUR

Good cooking, with an international flavour, at the restaurant in the hotel of the same name. *Hlíðarvegur 7 | tel. 4 87 80 50 | Moderate*

WHERE TO STAY

HVOLSVÖLLUR

Cosy hotel with a good range of amenities and friendly staff. The only source of accommodation in the town itself.

64 rooms | Hlíðarvegur 7 | tel. 4 87 80 50 | www.hotelhvolsvollur.is | Moderate

RANGÁ ●

Luxury with a fine view is on offer at this hotel with a country-house feel, situated 4km/2.5mi to the west of Hvolsvöllur. The INSIDER TIP seven themed suites are a big hit with visitors, but the standard rooms cater to all needs, too. *44 rooms, 7 suites | Suðurlandsvegur | tel. 4 78 57 00 | www.allseasonhotels.is | Expensive*

INFORMATION

TOURIST INFORMATION

At the Saga Centre. *Austurvegur 8 | tel. 4 87 80 43 | www.south.is | In summer, daily*

WHERE TO GO

HEKLA ★ (120 B4) *(H10)*

The most notoriously active volcano on Iceland is the 4km/2.5mi-long fissure vent, Hekla, 50km/31mi north-east of Hvolsvöllur. The 1491m/4655ft-high massif is visible from a distance and was considered the gateway to Hell until well into the 18th century. This was the only way people could explain the devastating blasts of fire and lava, such as the eruption in 1104 which wiped out a flourishing settlement in the Þjórsádalur valley. The many subsequent outbursts have turned the area around Hekla into an impressive lava-clad landscape. The easiest ascent is from the north and is rewarded by a stunning view across the highlands.

The *Hekla Centre* is an excellent source of information about the volcano and surrounding area *(daily 10am–9pm | At the Hótel Leirubakki on Rte. 26 | Admission: 800 ISK)*. The hotel has everything you need for a relaxing holiday, including *hot pot* and riding excursions *(18 rooms | tel. 4 87 87 00 | www.leirubakki.is | Moderate)*.

HLÍÐARENDI (120 B5) *(H11)*

The farm and what is supposedly the burial mound of Njál's friend Gunnar lie some 15km/9.3mi east of Hvolsvöllur INSIDER TIP in the picturesque *Fljótsdalur* valley, with its verdant slopes and many waterfalls. Instead of fleeing for his life, Gunnar, captivated by the beauty of his farm, remained in the country and was slain. From here, you have a fabulous view of the plain and the river, encircled by green sloping hills. The little church completes this idyllic picture-postcard scene.

ÞÓRSMÖRK ★ (120 B–C5) *(J11)*

Some 40km/25mi east of Hvolsvöllur at the end of the mountain road F 249 is the Þórsmörk valley in the foothills of three protective glaciers. Numerous hiking trails criss-cross the area which is ringed off by torrential glacier rivers and is popular with day-trippers due to its lush vegetation. There is a kiosk and a campsite. Starting in Þórsmörk, you can set off on a four-day trek to *Landmannalaugar* (120 C4) *(J10)* or hike in two days to *Skógar* (120 B5) *(J11)*. The Icelandic Touring Association *Ferðafélags Íslands (Fí | Reykjavík | Mörkin 6 | tel. 5 68 25 33 | www.fi.is)* and *Útivist (Reykjavík | Laugavegur 178 | tel. 5 62 10 00 | www.utivist.is)* offer guided hikes and accommodation in mountain huts.

SELFOSS

(119 F5) *(F10)* **The small town of Selfoss (5000 inh.) is the main trading centre of agricultural produce in the South. For years now, attempts have been made to expand the tourism industry here. Enjoy the countryside and the town on a walk along the Ölfusá river.**

One of the oldest dairies in Iceland is in Selfoss; it was opened in 1929. Not surprisingly, the local supermarkets have a selection of cheese specialities on their shelves. Selfoss is an ideal base for exploring south of the island.

FOOD & DRINK

KAFFI-KRÚS
Cosy and nostalgic, with fine pastries and cakes. *Austurvegur 7 | tel. 4 82 16 72 | Budget*

VIÐ FJÖRUBORÐIÐ ⚜
Famous for its king prawns and with a sensational view out to sea! *Eyrarbraut 3a | Stokkseyri | tel. 4 83 15 50 | Moderate–Expensive*

WHERE TO STAY

FOSSTÚN APARTMENT HOTEL
Centrally placed and well equipped. Although there is a kitchen in each apartment, you can also book breakfast if you wish. Ideal for families. *32 apartments | Eyrarvegur 26 | tel. 4 80 12 00 | www.fosstun.is | Moderate*

GESTHÚS
These little wooden houses, including kitchen and bathroom, are great for families. *22 cabins | Engjavegur | tel. 4 82 35 85 | www.gesthus.is | Budget*

INFORMATION

UPPLÝSINGAMIÐSTÖÐ ÁRBORG
In the local library. *May–Aug | Austurvegur 2 | tel. 4 82 19 90 | www.arborg.is*

WHERE TO GO

GEYSIR ★ (120 A3) (*𝕞 G9*)
The thermal area 65km/40mi to the north-east of Selfoss is the site of the *Great Geysir*, whose 14m/46ft-diameter pool is surrounded by fascinating sinter deposits. Just 100m/328ft away, the *Strokkur* geyser regularly spouts plumes of water into the air. Apart from these two springs, there are many smaller ones, whose colours cover a spectrum from turquoise to red, depending on the minerals occurring. The view over the area from INSIDER TIP ⚜ *Laugarfell* is particularly rewarding. A multimedia show at the *Geysir Center* informs visitors about the region. The *Hótel Geysir* is ideal for a longer stay *(24 rooms | tel. 4 80 68 00 | www.geysircenter.is | Budget–Moderate)*. Try the Icelandic buffet at the hotel restaurant *(Moderate)*.

The water spurts almost 20m/65ft into the air out of the Strokkur geyser

GULLFOSS ⭐ (120 B2) (𝔐 H9)

You'll find one of Iceland's most stunning waterfalls just 7km/4.4mi from the Great Geysir: the Gullfoss ('golden waterfall'). The glacial river Hvítá plunges down in twin cascades, at 90 degree to each other, into the *Hvítárgljúfur* gorge. The 31m/102ft-high waterfall and gorge were declared protected sites in 1979. There is an exhibition about Gullfoss at the upper car park, plus a shop and café.

SKÁLHOLT (120 A3) (𝔐 G9)

Halfway between Selfoss and Geysir is Skálholt, Bishop's seat from 1056 to 1756 and former cultural centre of the country. The crypt of the church, consecrated in 1963, contains the remains of the 44 bishops of Skálholt. A memorial to the north of the church harks back to the last Catholic bishop, Jón Arason. It stands on the spot on which he was beheaded by the Danes in 1550, together with his sons, for refusing to convert to Protestantism. There is a six-week season of INSIDER TIP concerts in July and August *(Information: tel. 4 86 88 24 | www.sumartonleikar.is)*.

VÍK Í MÝRDAL

(120 C6) (𝔐 J12) **Vík is the most southerly village in Iceland, whose 300 inhabitants live from trade and tourism. The village is situated at the foot of the ☀ Reynisfjall ridge (340m/1115ft) amidst green meadows and surrounded by black sandar plains and pebble beaches.**

The ● beaches at the foot of the Mýrdalsjökull rate amongst the most beautiful in the country; some feature basalt columns or accessible caves. Birdwatchers will find thousands of seabirds, such as Arctic tern and fulmar, which also nest here. The area offers great opportunities for walking in the immediate vicinity, both for experienced hikers as well as those who prefer a gentler stroll.

SIGHTSEEING

REYNISDRANGAR

Three rocky basalt stacks rise from the sea to the south of Reynisfjall, the highest of them measuring 66m/216ft. Legend has it that they were originally trolls who have been turned to stone. On the way there, you pass a INSIDER TIP memorial to the crews of German fishing trawlers who drowned in the waters off the south coast in the first half of the 20th century.

FOOD & DRINK

HALLDÓRSKAFFI

Cosy café in the historic house which is also home to the Tourist Information Of-

fice. *Vikurbraut 28 | tel. 4 87 12 02 |
Budget*

WHERE TO STAY

LUNDI
Small and cosy: from rooms with en-suite bathroom to sleeping-bag accom-modation. Good restaurant. *21 rooms |
Víkurbraut 26a | tel. 4 87 12 12 | www.ho
telpuffin.is | Budget–Moderate*

*4 87 85 00 | www.dyrholaey.com | Trip to
cape: 4500 ISK*

SKÓGAR ★ (120 B5) (*∅ J11*)
Around 32km/20mi west of Vík, an im-posing waterfall, *Skógafoss,* thunders 60m/197ft over the precipice into the valley below. When the sun shines, peo-ple say you can see the shimmering chest of gold hidden behind the water-fall by Skógar's first settlers. When a boy

Perfect protection against the icy winter winds:
turf-roofed houses at the open-air museum in Skógar

INFORMATION

TOURIST INFORMATION BRYDEBÚÐ
*15 June–Aug | Vikurbraut 28 | tel.
4 87 13 95 | www.vik.is*

WHERE TO GO

DYRHÓLAEY ☼ (120 C6) (*∅ J12*)
The promontory to the west of Vík rises 120m/395ft. out of the sea and takes its name – literally 'door hole island' – from its gaping archway. A lighthouse, built in 1910, stands on the cape. You can drive to the archway along the beach in am-phibious vehicles. *Dyhólaeyjarferðir | tel.*

once tried to fetch the chest, he only managed to grab the handle, which is now on show at the *Skógar Folk Museum
(June–Aug daily 9am–6pm, May/Sept
10am–5pm, Oct–April 11am–4pm | Café:
June–Aug daily 10am–5pm | Admission:
1200 ISK | www.skogasafn.is)*. This is the most impressive museum of its kind on Iceland, describing, among other things, the history of island transport.
The stylish *Hótel Skógar (12 rooms | tel.
4 87 48 80 | www.hotelskogar.is | Expen-sive)* has ☼ a number of rooms with a view of the waterfall. Good restau-rant.

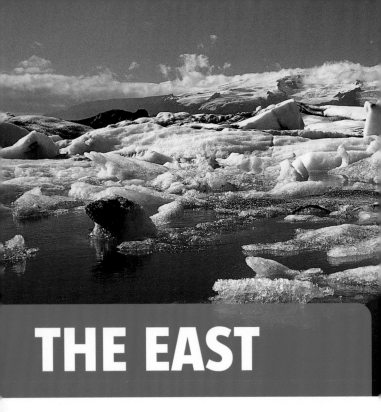

THE EAST

The countryside in the East has two distinct faces – on the one hand, the area to the south of the Vatnajökull glacier from the Skeiðarársandur sandar to Höfn and, on the other, the fjord landscape of the east coast, with its steep, towering basalt ridges.

These formations consist of the oldest types of rock on the island. Basalt, easily recognisable by its column-like structure, dominates, but the somewhat surreal colour spectrum of the mountains – dependent on climatic and light conditions – is down to the presence of rhyolite.

Traditionally, settlements were – and still are – based on trade and fishing; farming is only possible to a limited extent, due to the lack of suitable space. Today, the small coastal villages and towns are fighting for survival as young people in particular are flocking to the towns. It is hoped the region will be revitalised thanks to the aluminium smelting plant in Reyðarfjörður. The necessary electricity comes from the Kárahnjúkar hydroelectric plant, for which an area of 57km²/22mi² north-east of Vatnajökull has been flooded and two glacial rivers diverted through a tunnel.

Large tracts of land to the south of Vatnajökull have silted up under the endless stream of deposits transported by the glacier meltwater. Regular volcanic eruptions underneath the ice cap lead to glacial bursts which, over the centuries, have transformed this once green swathe of land into a stony wilderness, the sandar. The most recent and power-

Photo: Ice on the Jökulsárlón glacial lake

Between glaciers and fjords: the fascinating world of the Vatnajökull ice cap and old, idyllic trading posts

ful glacial flood took place in 1996, destroying the bridge and a section of the Ring Road on Skeiðarársandur.

DJÚPIVOGUR

(123 E3) *(∅ R7)* **Old houses and a small marina characterise the face of this over 400-year-old trading post, whose 350 inhabitants still live from fishing.**

In the centre, you'll find the 200-year-old *Langabúð*, a former log warehouse now housing a museum and café, and, next door to it, the cooperative building from the 19th century. The old part of the hotel also dates back to this period. In the summer, the area is populated by countless birds. The *Búlandsnes* promontory, peppered with lakes, is a designated birdwatching site; a number of signs have been erected with information on what you can expect to see. *www.birds.is* The INSIDER TIP stone eggs by artist Sigurður Guðmundsson erected around the harbour *Gleðivík* are an attractive addition to the vil-

Splash of colour in a barren landscape: a stone wall protects this farm near Djúpivogur

lage. Thirty-four of these stone sculptures in the shape of birds' eggs stand along the coast. The coloured, polished natural stones resemble the real things, laid by the species native to the area around Djúpivogur – they're just a lot bigger!

SIGHTSEEING

LANGABUÐ
Works by sculptor Ríkarður Jónsson and a collection in memory of politician Eysteinn Jónsson are to be found here. Both men hail from the region. *June–Aug daily 10am–6pm | Admission: 500 ISK*

WHERE TO STAY

FRAMTÍÐ
Sauna, solarium and large rooms with shower/WC. In the older part of the hotel, the rooms are more modest. The *restaurant* specialises in fish. *46 rooms |*

Vogaland 4 | tel. 4 78 88 87 | www.simnet. is/framtid | Moderate

INFORMATION

LANGABUÐ
June–Aug only | Tel. 4 78 82 20 | www. djupivogur.is

WHERE TO GO

INSIDER TIP ▶ **PAPEY** ⚲ (123 E3) (*𝄌 R8*)
Until the year 900 AD, Irish monks lived on the largest of the islands off Djúpivogur; you can still see ruins from the period and an abandoned farm. Papey is an ideal destination for birdwatching. *June– 15 Sept | 2-hr trip with guide: 5500 ISK | Papeyjarferðir | tel. 4 78 88 38 | papey@ djupivogur.is*

TEIGARHORN (123 E3) (*𝄌 R7*)
Four kilometres (2.5mi) away, there is a nature reserve named after the Teigarhorn farm at the foot of the pyramid-shaped basalt mountain *Búlandstindur* (1069m/3507ft). The spot is well known as a source of beautiful stones and minerals. It is now forbidden, however, for visitors to collect minerals. Around 1900, the site was also the location of the atelier of Iceland's first female photographer, Nicoline Weywadt (1848–1921).

EGILSSTAÐIR

(117 E5) (*𝄌 R5*) **Around 2300 people live in the only proper town in the region, which has developed into a commercial centre since its founding in 1944.** Not surprisingly, the state forestry commission office has its headquarters here, close to the Hallormsstaður forest. Egilsstaðir is a good place to start for trips into the forest, the eastern high-

lands, the small coastal villages as well as to the Lagarfljót lake (also known as Lögurinn). Over the years, a lively cultural scene has grown up, featuring an opera studio, theatre group and jazz club. The INSIDER TIP far north-east of Iceland is a real insider tip: the *Melrakkaslétta* plain and tiny coastal settlements such as *Raufarhöfn* (116 C1) *(ⁿ O1)* or *Vopnafjörður* (117 D4) *(ⁿ Q4)* are well worth a closer look. The latter were once prosperous fishing villages, also with rich supplies of driftwood; today, they are fighting to survive. Only few tourists make it out here, often having the strip of land along the coast all to themselves. In the villages, however, there is plenty of accommodation available and a broad spectrum of activities on offer. www.visitnortheasticeland.is

SIGHTSEEING

MINJASAFN AUSTURLANDS
The *East Iceland Heritage Museum* documents life in the region from the time of settlement down to the 19th century. Star exhibit is the grave of a man, complete with his horse and various personal effects, dating back to the year 980, which was uncovered in the Þórisá river in 1995. *Mon–Thu 11am–9pm, Fri–Sun 11am–5pm | Admission: 500 ISK, Wed: free | Laufskógar 1 | www.minjasafn.is*

FOOD & DRINK

EDDA ☼
International dishes with an Icelandic touch. Located in the hotel of the same name, it has fine views across the pretty Lagarfljót lake. *Tjarnarbraut 25 | tel. 4 44 48 80 | Moderate*

KAFFI NIELSEN
In the evenings, the mood is Italian; in the afternoons, it's time for cake! Sit on the terrace in summer. *Tjarnarbraut 1 | tel. 4 71 26 26 | Budget–Moderate*

A little Icelander! What else?

SPORTS & ACTIVITIES

You can get information about hikes, boat trips and riding excursions as well as fishing licences from the East Iceland Information Centre (see p. 56).
Golfers should head 5km/3.1mi to the north-west for a leisurely round at *Fljótdalshérað (tel. 4 71 11 13 | www.golf.is/gfh)* near Fellabær.

★ **Hallormsstaður**
Iceland's one and only 'proper' forest is by the Lagarfljót lake
→ p. 56

★ **Jökulsárlón**
Cruise on a boat between shimmering blue and green icebergs
→ p. 59

★ **Skaftafell**
At the foot of Iceland's largest glacier, Vatnajökull, in the National Park of the same name, is a green paradise of walking trails, hot springs and glacier tongues → p. 59

MARCO POLO HIGHLIGHTS

EGILSSTAÐIR

ENTERTAINMENT

In June there's a popular jazz festival, featuring artists from Iceland and Scandinavia. www.east.is

WHERE TO STAY

EDDA

Central location. Some of the spacious rooms are over two floors; ideal for families. *52 rooms | Tjarnarbraut 25 | tel. 4 44 48 80 | www.hoteledda.is | Budget–Moderate*

INSIDER TIP **VÍNLAND GUEST HOUSE** ☆
Tastefully furnished and equipped with fridge and tea- and coffee-making facilities. Internet access, too. Some rooms have a lovely view of the sea. Free transport to the airport. *6 rooms | Fellabæ | tel. 6 15 19 00 | www.vinland-gisting.net | Moderate*

INFORMATION

EAST ICELAND INFORMATION CENTRE
Miðvangur 1–3 | tel. 4 71 23 20 | www.east.is

LOW BUDGET

▶ Just 15km/9.3mi from Vopnafjörður is *Selárdalur*, a small, romantic, freely accessible ● thermal swimming pool. Variously illuminated by candlelight, moonlight or the fascinating Northern Lights. *Daily 7am–11pm | tel. 4 73 14 99*

▶ Value-for-money food is on the table at the lively service station restaurant *Söluskáli-Hraðbúð (Kaupvangur | tel. 4 70 12 00)* in Egilsstaðir.

WHERE TO GO

HALLORMSSTAÐUR ★ (117 D6) (*∅ Q6*)
Iceland's largest woodland and reafforestation area, with a stock of trees up to 100 years old, lies 12 km to the south. Take a fascinating walk through the educational forest in which a broad range of conifers and deciduous trees grow. Thanks to the favourable soil conditions and the almost continental climate, the trees enjoy ideal growing conditions. The *Hotel Hallormsstaður (35 rooms | tel. 47 24 00 | www.hotel701.is | Moderate)* is quiet and prettily situated. In addition, there are wooden cabins and a more modest guest house. Riding excursions are also offered. The beautiful ● INSIDER TIP *Atlavík campsite* is for the romantic at heart; here, you can sleep under the trees, directly by the shore of Lagarfljót lake.

LAGARFLJÓT
(117 D–E 4–6) (*∅ Q–R 4–6*)
Three kilometres (1.86mi) wide and around 30km/18.6mi long, the lake is fed by a number of glacial rivers and narrows to form the Lagarfljót river. Legend has it that a giant worm-like monster, Lagarfljótsormurinn, lives on the bed of the lake! During the summer, you can take a boat trip between Egilsstaðir and the Atlavík campsite. Incidentally, the boat is even named after Nessie's Icelandic cousin! *Lagarfljótsormurinn | tel. 4 71 29 00 | Trip: 3000 ISK*

SEYÐISFJÖRÐUR (117 F5) (*∅ R5*)
If you arrive by ferry, the picturesque village of 700 inhabitants, 27km/17mi east of Egilsstaðir, is your first point of contact with Iceland. In the 19th century, this used to be the country's largest commercial settlement, and the well preserved wooden houses date back to this period.

Fish trawler in the only harbour on the south-east coast, at Höfn

Alongside a broad cultural programme, including museums and summer concerts, Seyðisfjörður is a good starting point for hikes in the eastern fjord region. The small INSIDER TIP *Hótel Aldan (9 rooms | Norðurgata 2 | tel. 4 72 12 77 | Moderate)*, a mixture of creature comforts and nostalgia, is located in one of the historic houses.

SKRIÐUKLAUSTUR (117 D6) (⟨∅⟩ *Q6*)

A monastery stood here, on the south-west bank of the Lagarfljót, in the 16th century. In 1939, author Gunnar Gunnarsson built himself a 1000m²/10764ft² house to plans by German architect Fritz Höger. Today, it is home to a cultural centre which, among other things, stages exhibitions about Gunnarsson and also has a great café. *Tel. 4 71 29 90 | www. skriduklaustur.is*

VÉGARÐUR (117 D6) (⟨∅⟩ *Q6*)

Landsvirkjun, the state power company, has set up an information centre here on the subject of the most controversial power plant project in the country, *Kárah-njúkar HEP*. Construction of the 57km² /22mi² *Hálslón reservoir* (122 C2)

(⟨∅⟩ *O7*) on the north-eastern edge of Vatnajökull has meant the destruction of a part of the Dimmugljúfur gorge. The power plant itself is situated a little to the south of Végarður. *May–Oct daily 9am–5pm | Turn-off from Rte. 931 (signposted) | tel. 4 71 20 44 | www.karahnjukar.is*

HÖFN

(123 D4) (⟨∅⟩ *Q9*) **This village of around 1600 inhabitants, whose name simply means 'harbour', is the administrative and commercial centre for the communities in the south-east.**

Located in a picturesque setting at the foot of the Vatnajökull ice cap, Höfn – or to give it its full name Höfn í Hornafjörður – was a trading post in the 19th century. Some old buildings from the time still stand on the harbour and today house the *Folk Museum*. There is also a small shopping centre. Close to the harbour, you'll find the *recreation area* and the ☺ INSIDER TIP *Ósland Bird Sanctuary*, home to the great northern diver, Arctic tern and whooper swan.

SIGHTSEEING

JÖKLASÝNING (GLACIER EXHIBITION)
Bags of information about glaciers, the Vatnajökull in particular, from a scientific, artistic and historical point of view. One of the best multimedia museums in the country. *May–Sept daily 10am–6pm | Admission: 1000 ISK | Vöruhús | Hafnarbraut 30 | www.is-land.is*

FOOD & DRINK

CAFÉS
For a quick bite in between, try the café in the shopping centre or the one at the Nautical Museum, *Pakkhúsið (Budget).*

INSIDER TIP KAFFI HORNIÐ
Cosy, down-to-earth atmosphere and a good selection of fish and meat dishes (à la carte and daily specials). *Hafnarbraut 42 | tel. 4 78 26 00 | Budget–Moderate*

WHERE TO STAY

ÁSGARÐUR
Attractive location by the sea and next to the Ósland Bird Sanctuary. Unfussy rooms with shower/WC. *36 rooms | Ránarslóð 3 | tel. 4 78 13 65 | Moderate*

BOOKS & FILMS

▶ **The Atom Station** – The novel by Nobel prize-winner, Halldór Laxness, reflects the unease in Iceland when the Icelandic Parliament decided in 1946 to allow the USA to set up a base at the Keflavík airfield. (First published in 1948)

▶ **Independent People** – Also by Laxness, this epic novel tells the story of life in rural Iceland of the early 20th century, a far cry from today's ultra-hip Reykjavík, but well worth reading for its black humour and sharp characterisation. (First published in 1946)

▶ **Volcano Island** – Pictures of Iceland and the changed glacial landscape following the eruption of Eyjafjallajökull in 2011, captured by renowned photographer Sigurgeir Sigurjónsson.

▶ **Iceland (Classic Geology in Europe)** – Let Thor Thordarson and Armann Hoskuldsson fill you in with some background information on what Iceland is really made of – literally. (2002)

▶ **Iceland Sagas** – Magnus Magnusson explores the legendary tales which form Iceland's cultural heritage in their historical and geographic context. (2005)

▶ **101 Reykjavík** – Film of the same-name cult novel by Hallgrimur Helgason with plenty of music, off-beat humour and crazy characters. Directed by Baltasar Kormákur. (2000)

▶ **Iceland 63°66°N** – Stefan Erdmann's three films are an invitation to immerse yourself in some beautiful images. The aerial pictures give you the impression of looking at a painting. Excellent soundtrack, also in English. (2 DVDs, 2011)

▶ **Screaming Masterpiece** – The film (DVD) for lovers of Icelandic music: a 2005 documentation including loads of concert clips.

HÖFN
Top hotel in town, centrally located and with all amenities. There's a decent restaurant, too. *68 rooms | Vikurbraut 24 | tel. 4 78 12 40 | Expensive*

UPPLÝSINGAMIÐSTÖÐ FERÐAMANNA
Tourist information office at the Glacier Exhibition. *Hafnarbraut 30 | tel. 4 78 15 00 | www.rikivatnajokuls.is*

recharge your batteries at the *restaurant (15 May–15 Sept | tel. 4 78 21 22 | Budget)* with its fine view across the lagoon.

SKAFTAFELL ★ ☺ (122 A5) (⬚ N10)
Right in the middle of the Vatnajökull National Park – at 13,600 km^2/5250mi^2, the largest in Europe – is the green idyll of Skaftafell which extends between the icy tongues of the Morsárjökull and Skaftafellsjökull glaciers. Over 210 species of plant grow in the region, its microclimate

Sometimes the path turns out to be a river: hiking in Skaftafell National Park

WHERE TO GO

JÖKULSÁRLÓN ★ (122 B5) (⬚ O10)
The *Breiðamerkurjökull* glacier calves into this 200m/656ft-deep lake, 75km/46mi south-west of Höfn; the scene is one of countless blue-black icebergs drifting across the backdrop of the Vatnajökull. Enjoy some fascinating perspectives on a boat trip on the lagoon, right up close to these bizarre formations. This breathtaking setting is popular with film-makers, not least those behind the James Bond movies. Information and bookings: *tel. 4 78 21 22 | www.glacierlagoon.com*. After your trip, you can have a bite to eat and

protected by the Öræfajökull glacier; bird life, too, is plentiful and varied.
There are many hiking trails criss-crossing the park, 135km/84mi to the west of Höfn. Popular spots with visitors are the *Svartifoss* waterfall and ⛰ the *Sjónarsker* observation point, facing out over the glacier and the desert-like plain, the Skeiðarársandur. You can also take part in a guided hike up Iceland's highest mountain, *Hvannadalshnúkur* (2119m/6952ft). Information is to be had at the *Service Centre (tel. 4 78 33 00 | May–Sept)* in the park. Inside the park, there is only one campsite and the guest house *Bölti (5 rooms, 2 huts | tel. 4 78 16 26 | Budget)*.

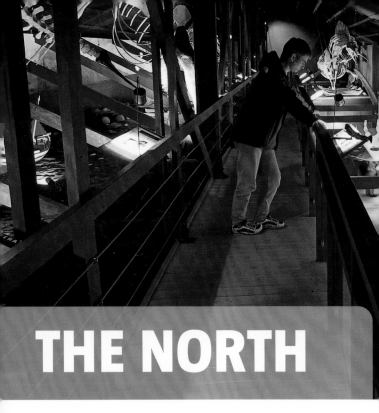

THE NORTH

The northern region is a chequered landscape stretching from the northwestern fjords right up into the highlands. One of the most impressive areas in terms of geology and scenery is the Mývatn region, with its many spectacular natural features.

The main centre of population in the North is Akureyri, a charming little town which has been striving in recent years to turn itself into a mini-metropolis. The many historic sites dotted around Skagafjörður are worth a look; in previous centuries, major trading centres and Iceland's second bishopric were located here. The Skagafjörður region is also famous for horse-breeding – some local studs have an excellent reputation abroad.

AKUREYRI

(115 E3) *(ĎJ L4)* Iceland's fourth-largest municipality lies in an attractive spot in the Eyjafjörður region at the foot of Súlur (1144m/1251ft). From the summit, you have a great view of the hinterland and the fjord.

The 17,500 residents live from trade, food production as well as shipbuilding. Akureyri is not only the main tourist centre, but also the cultural heart of the North. In 1975, a professional theatre was founded in the town, now at home in a fine wooden building dating back to 1900. Iceland's second university opened its doors to students in 1987. The town owes much of its charm to its many old

Photo: Sperm whale skeleton at the Whale Museum in Húsavík

Hot springs and a wealth of history: the varied face of Iceland's North cannot fail to impress

villas and profusion of trees and is often titled the 'Pearl of the North'.

SIGHTSEEING

AKUREYRARKIRKJA

A most striking church building for which the architect Guðjón Samúelsson looked to Iceland's typical basalt columns for inspiration. The 17 church windows, illustrating events from the history of Icelandic Christianity, are an interesting feature. One window in particular stands out; it was originally part of Coventry Cathedral in England and is 400 years old. *June–Aug Mon–Fri 10am–5pm | Concerts on Sundays in July*

LYSTIGARÐURINN (BOTANICAL GARDEN) ●

The garden was originally laid out in 1912 and is the most northerly of its kind. It contains all of Iceland's native plants (approximately 430 species) and almost 6000 others from various regions, for example, Greenland or even Southern

Europe. *June–Sept Mon–Fri 8am–10pm, Sat/Sun 9am–10pm | Free admission | Eyrarlandsvegur*

HOF CULTURAL AND CONFERENCE CENTRE

The eye-catching Menningarhúsið HOF was opened in 2010. A circular structure with a generously proportioned interior, its façade is clad with slabs of dark green basalt. It is the setting for regular exhibi-

NONNAHÚS

The town's most famous son is Jesuit priest and children's writer Jón Sveinsson (affectionately known as 'Nonni') who lived with his family in this house from 1850 onwards. He is widely known in continental Europe for his 'Nonni books', which centre on his childhood and experiences with his brother, 'Manni'. *June–Aug daily 10am–5pm | Admission: 500 ISK | Aðalstræti 54a | www.nonni.is*

Only 15m/50ft high, but still a real stunner: horseshoe-shaped Goðafoss

tions as well as a varied programme of music and theatre performances. There's also a good restaurant with a terrace directly on the waterfront. Alongside salads, pasta and fish dishes, they also serve cakes and snacks. *Strandgata 12 | tel. 4 50 10 00 | www.menningarhus.is | Budget–Moderate*

LISTASAFN IN THE LISTAGIL

This particular road, Kaupvangsstræti, has acquired a nickname, 'Listagil' ('Art Valley'). In addition to a number of galleries, it is also the site of *Akureyri Art Museum*. Changing exhibitions feature mostly Icelandic artists of the 20th century. *Tue–Sun noon–5pm | Free admission | Kaupvangsstræti 24 | www.listasafn.akureyri.is*

FOOD & DRINK

BAUTIN

Good restaurant with a nostalgic feel to it and a wide range of dishes. As well as whale and horse meat specialities, there's a reasonably priced salad bar. *Hafnarstræti 92 | tel. 4 62 18 18 | Budget–Moderate*

INSIDER TIP ▶ BLÁA KANNAN

Cosy, popular café in the main shopping street selling snacks and cakes. *Hafnarstræti 96 | tel. 4 61 46 00 | Budget*

KAFFI KARÓLÍNA

Cool, artists' hang-out in 'Art Valley'. Relaxed atmosphere. There's a top-of-the-range restaurant, RUB 23, under the same roof. *Kaupvangsstræti 23 | tel. 461 27 55 | Budget–Moderate*

SPORTS & ACTIVITIES

Ferðafélag Akureyrar (Strandgata 23 | tel. 4 62 27 20 | www.ffa.est.is) offers guided hikes in the area. Akureyri also has some great ski runs in the winter *(information: www.hlidarfjall.is)* and there's even an ice rink *(Naustavegur)*.

WHERE TO STAY

ÍBÚÐIR
Six large, fully equipped apartments, with balcony. *Geislagata 10 | tel. 8 92 98 38 | www.hotelibudir.is | Moderate*

SÆLUHÚS
Surrounded by green fields, 33 bright, modern apartments. Some even have their own hot pot. *Sunnutröð 2 | tel. 6 18 28 00 | www.saeluhus.is | Moderate*

STÓRHOLT
Hostel in the middle of town, with garden and hot pot. There are 70 beds in rooms of various sizes, plus two bungalows sleeping eight. *Stórholt 1 | tel. 4 62 36 57 | www.akureyrihostel.com | Budget*

INFORMATION

TOURIST INFORMATION
15 June–Aug | Menningarhúsið HOF | Strandgata 12 | tel. 4 50 10 50 | www.visit akureyri.is

WHERE TO GO

GOÐAFOSS (119 F3) (*Ø M4*)
Some 50km/31mi to the east of Akureyri, the Goðafoss waterfall cascades over a broad precipice. It acquired its name 'Waterfall of the Gods', in the year 1000, when all statues of the heathen gods were flung into the waters following the adoption of Christianity. Accommodation is to be had nearby, too: *Fosshóll (26 rooms | tel. 4 64 31 08 | www.nett.is/ fossholl | Budget–Moderate)*.

GRÍMSEY (0) (*Ø L1*)
The flight to Iceland's northernmost point takes 20 minutes: the remote island of Grímsey lies on the Arctic Circle (66° 30' North) and is 41km/25mi from the mainland. Every visitor receives a certificate to document his visit. The towering 100m/328ft-high cliffs are a paradise for birdwatchers. Some 30 species of seabird populate the rocks. *Air Iceland | 14,590 ISK | tel. 4 60 70 00 | www.airiceland.is*

MÝVATNS-SVEIT

(116 A4) (*Ø M–N 4*) **The community around Mývatn lake numbers 400 in-**

MARCO POLO HIGHLIGHTS

MÝVATNS-SVEIT

habitants. Mývatn, including the largest settlement, Reykjahlíð in the North, is a favourite with tourists.

The Krafla geothermal power plant also plays an important role in the region which is part of an active volcanic zone and experiences frequent eruptions.

SIGHTSEEING

DIMMUBORGIR (116 A4) (ひ N4)

The lava formations at Dimmuborgir have a fabulous, other-worldly character. Here, you'll come across tunnels and caves with names like *kirkjan,* 'The Church'. In the summer, you can take a seat on INSIDER TIP 'Father Christmas's Chair'. Some of the lava sculptures piled up amidst lush vegetation are 40m/131ft high. The ⋇ Hverfjall crater to the north has a diameter of 1km/0.62mi and is 140m/460ft deep, making it the biggest in Iceland. The entire area is a protected nature reserve.

MÝVATN ★ (160 A4) (ひ M–N4)

Iceland's fourth-biggest lake is characterised by fascinating lava formations and rich vegetation along its banks. As well as other birds, over 15 species of duck breed here in large colonies, drawn by the favourable climate and plentiful supply of mosquito (larvae), from which the lake takes its name. They may be annoying, but at least they don't bite. Numerous springs issue from the bottom of the lake which has a maximum depth of 5m/16ft. Its only outlet is the *Laxá,* a well-known salmon river.

The fine INSIDER TIP *Fuglasafn Sigurgeirs* (Bird Museum) *(15 May–Aug daily 11am–7pm | Admission: 800 ISK | www.fuglas afn.is),* featuring stuffed specimens of regional birdlife, stands on the northwest bank. The atmosphere in this thoroughly modern showcase, though, is anything but stuffy! ⋇ Café overlooking the lake.

NÁMASKARÐ ● (116 A4) (ひ N4)

An expanse of solfataras cloaks the base of ⋇ Námafjall (482m/1581ft), each of the many steaming fumeroles belching out sulphur from the springs below. The temperature of the mud pots can reach 100 °C/212°F, and the lighter-coloured parts of the surface crust can cave in easily. Sulphur was extracted here for hundreds of years for use in the manufacture of gunpowder.

Bubbling, steaming and hissing – and it smells, too: Námaskarð solfatara field

FOOD & DRINK

GAMLI BÆRINN (116 A4) (*N4*)
The old farmhouse is now a cosy café, serving cakes and light bites. *Reykjahlíð | tel. 4 64 42 70 | Budget*

GÍGUR ᨶ (116 A4) (*M4*)
Restaurant in the same-name hotel with a fantastic view of the lake. Exquisite food. *Skútustaðir | tel. 4 64 44 55 | Expensive*

SPORTS & ACTIVITIES

Just float away and daydream in turquoise-blue, mineral-rich water surrounded by lava fields – there can be hardly a more beautiful place to do so than the lagoon at Mývatn and the INSIDER TIP Nature Baths which were opened in 2004. *June–Aug daily 9am–midnight, Sept–May noon–10pm | Admission: 2500 ISK | www.jardbodin.is*

WHERE TO STAY

FERÐAÞJÓNUSTA HLÍÐ
(116 A4) (*N4*)
Modest rooms and sleeping-bag accommodation. The six four-bed cabins and the four bungalows are a pretty alternative. *13 rooms | Reykjahlíð | Hraunbrún | tel. 4 64 41 03 | hlidmyv.is | Budget*

REYKJAHLÍÐ (116 A4) (*N4*)
This small hotel directly on the lake has been tastefully renovated. *9 rooms | Reykjahlíð | tel. 4 64 41 42 | www.reykjahlid.is | Expensive*

SEL-HÓTEL MÝVATN (116 A4) (*M4*)
Very well equipped, tastefully furnished and with a view of the lake. Bikes for hire. Plenty of INSIDER TIP activities in winter. *35 rooms | Skútustaðir | tel. 4 64 41 64 | www.myvatn.is | Expensive*

INFORMATION

INFORMATION CENTRE
(116 A4) (*N4*)
Hraunvegur 8 | Reykjalíð | tel. 4 64 43 90 | www.myv.is

WHERE TO GO

DETTIFOSS ★ (116 B3) (*N–O4*)
Around 40km/25mi to the north-east of Mývatn, Mother Nature has crafted a gigantic, 100m/328ft-wide waterfall. The sheer mass of water from the glacial river Jökulsá á Fjöllum, which plunges 44m/144ft into the deep, is such that the surrounding area is enveloped in a cloud of spray lit up by dazzling rainbows.

HÚSAVÍK (115 F1) (*M3*)
The main attractions in this prettily situated fishing village, 60km/37mi to the north of Mývatn, are the *whale-watching tours (North Sailing | tel. 4 64 23 50 | www.northsailing.is)* on restored oak vessels and the *Whale Museum (Hafnerstétt | June–Aug 9am–7pm, May/Sept 10am–5pm | Admission: 1000 ISK | www.whalemuseum.is)* which gives you bags of information on the different species of whale. Information on accommodation: *Tourist Information Centre (June–15 Sept | Hafnarstétt 1 | tel. 4 64 43 00 | www.visit northeasticeland.is)*.

JÖKULSÁRGLJÚFUR NATIONAL PARK ★ (116 B3) (*N3–4*)
The National Park reaches from Dettifoss – 40km/25mi north-east of Mývatn – for over 30km/18mi as far as Rte. 85 to the north and is today a part of the large Vatnajökull National Park. The 25km/15.5mi-long and up to 120m/394ft-deep *Jökulsárgljúfur* canyon, into which several waterfalls spill their load, is breathtaking. A hiking trail leads along the gorge to the

VARMAHLÍÐ

Vesturdalur valley some 16km/10mi away. Close by, you'll find the *Hlóðaklettar* basalt formations, nicknamed the 'Echoing Rocks'. From Vesturdalur, a further day's hike takes you through lush vegetation to *Ásbyrgi* (116 B3) *(ᐱ N3)*, a horseshoe-shaped, thickly wooded ravine with steep sides stretching up almost 100m/328ft. It is said to get its shape from the hoof-print left by Odin's eight-legged horse, Sleipnir. There are campsites at Vesturdalur and Ásbyrgi *(tel. 4 70 71 00 | www.vip.is)*.

VARMAHLÍÐ

(114 C3) *(ᐱ J4–5)* **This tiny village of 140 inhabitants has always been a busy stopover for travellers; today, it's a great starting point for your exploration of the Skagafjörður region.**

This part of Iceland is famous for its horses and has many historically significant places to visit. Standing on ☀ *Reykjarhóll* (111m/364ft) gives you a panoramic view of the entire area.

LOW BUDGET

▶ Whether you're looking for excitement, a waterside site with boat hire or a quiet spot in the lava fields, the three campsites in *Reykjahlíð* in *Mývatn* have value-for-money accommodation for everyone. *900 ISK per person*

▶ You can take the ferry to Grímsey from Dalvík for just 2800 ISK. *Mon, Wed, Fri | one-way trip: 3.5 hrs | tel. 4 58 89 70 | www.saefari.is*

FOOD & DRINK

GRILL
Service station and supermarket – and a good place to eat when you're on the road. The menu includes Icelandic hamburgers, sandwiches and hot dogs. *Budget*

VARMAHLÍÐ
Fine restaurant in the hotel of the same name. Local produce is the first choice when putting the menus together; not only the lamb and fish, but also the Mozzarella and other cheeses come from the region. *Tel. 4 53 81 70 | Moderate–Expensive*

WHERE TO STAY

HOTEL TINDASTÓLL 1884
The oldest hotel in Iceland – perhaps INSIDERTIP you can sleep in Marlene Dietrich's old room! Excellent facilities and furnishings. *10 rooms | Sauðárkrókur | Lindargata 3 | tel. 4 53 50 02 | www.hoteltindastoll.com | Moderate–Expensive*

INFORMATION

TOURIST INFORMATION
At the bus station. *Tel. 4 55 61 61 | www.visitskagafjordur.is*

WHERE TO GO

DRANGEY (114 B2) *(ᐱ H3)*
The steep cliffs of the tuff island of Drangey tower some 200m/656ft out of the middle of the Skagafjörður fjord. Many species of bird, such as guillemot, build their nests here again today; numbers at the seabird colonies have now recovered. In times of famine – especially in the 18th and 19th centuries – people used to hunt the birds, above all to plunder their

nests. In one spring, up to 200,000 birds are said to have been slaughtered. Today, visitors come here only to watch our feathered friends. Saga hero Grettir fled here, and legend has it he swam across the fjord in the process. Don't worry; you won't be subjected to such an ordeal! Information on conventional crossings: *Fagranes farm (4–5 hrs: 4000 ISK | tel. 4536310).*

GLAUMBÆR (114 C3) (*J4*)

Situated 7km/4.3mi north of Varmahlíð, this turf farm dating back to the 18th

left behind. *June–Aug daily 11am–6pm | Admission: 1500 ISK | www.hofsos.is*

HÓLAR ★ (114 C3) (*J4*)

Iceland's second bishop's seat (1106–1798) lies 30km/18.6mi to the north-east and is also the site of the oldest stone church on the island. It was consecrated in 1763, and the altar features an impressive triptych from the late Middle Ages. Hólar also boasts the first printing press in the country (1530), on which the first complete Icelandic translation of the Bible was printed in 1584.

Not Hobbiton, but Glaumbær: turf houses protect against the Icelandic climate

century has now been turned into a museum. Here, you can get an impression of living conditions in such dwellings which were typical for Iceland well into the 19th century. *June–10 Sept daily 9am–6pm | Admission: 600 ISK | www.glaumbaer.is*

HOFSÓS (114 C2) (*J3*)

The old trading post, 40km/25mi to the north, is home to the *Icelandic Emigration Centre.* From the beginning of the 19th century, thousands of Icelanders set sail for the New World in search of a better life for themselves. Often, what they found was no better than what they had

The former *Agricultural College* is now a University College specialising in equine science and tourism and also aquaculture and fish biology, which are taught in *Sauðárkrókur.* The old school house contains the *Icelandic Horse Centre,* tracing the history of this unique breed. An adjacent building houses a *freshwater aquarium (free admission to both attractions).* With a number of hiking trails and good places to stay, Hólar is a popular destination for holidaymakers in summer. You can stay in cottages and apartments or in sleeping-bag accommodation on the college *campus (tel. 4556333 | www. holar.is | Budget–Moderate).*

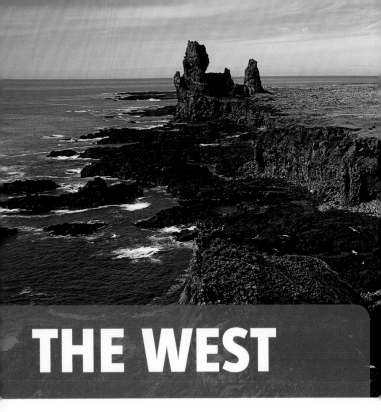

THE WEST

Three regions which could hardly be more fascinating make up the West of Iceland. Firstly, there's the area between Borgarnes and Langjökull – with farmland, hot springs, lava caves and lots of places which hark back to saga hero Egill Skallagrímsson.

Further north, the Snæfellsnes Peninsula features the mysterious Snæfellsjökull glacier at its western tip. Centuries ago, the coast was dotted with fishing villages; today the north coast has just a few larger ones, of which Stykkishólmur is the most important. In the far north-west, the saw-toothed coast of the Westfjords claws the sea; inland, an unparalleled landscape of stark beauty and utter seclusion is a paradise for birdwatchers and hikers. The main town is Ísafjörður, educational and cultural centre of the Westfjords, a region upon which a continual stream of residents has turned its back since the 1950s. The farms and villages here were too remote, accessible only over steep mountain passes.

BORGARNES

(119 D3) *(∅ E8)* **Despite its pretty much ideal location on the sea, the 1800 inhabitants live from trade and processing of agricultural produce.**

Hot water in the town emanates from the largest hot-water spring in Iceland, *Deildartunguhver*, some 33km/20mi away. The town, which was founded in 1867, seems rather sterile, despite its fine location. Its charm lies, above all, in the fact

Photo: Steep coastline of the Snæfellsjökull National Park

Sagas, beaches and seafarers: on the trail of Egill Skallagrímsson into the bleak, lonely north-west

that you stumble across traces of Egil's Saga Skallagrímssonar everywhere you go.

SIGHTSEEING

LANDNÁMSSETUR

The Settlement Centre opened in 2006 and showcases the story of the settlement of Iceland and Egil's Saga. Outstanding exhibition rooms, featuring clever use of modern lighting design. *June–Aug daily 10am–7pm, Sept–May daily 11am–5pm | Admission: 2400 ISK* *(for both exhibitions) | Brákarbraut 13–15 | www.landnam.is*

SKALLAGRÍMSGARÐUR

This pretty park lies in the centre of town and is the site of the burial mound under which Egill's father, Skallagrímur Kvéldúlfsson, is said to lie. The first settler was laid to rest in the Viking tradition with his horse and weapons. Nearby, a relief shows Egill carrying his drowned son, Böðvar, who also lies under the burial mound, according to the saga.

FOOD & DRINK

BÚÐARKLETTUR
Welcoming restaurant located in an old warehouse directly next to the Settlement Centre. The food's good, too. *Brákarbraut 13–15 | tel. 4 37 16 00 | Moderate*

heading north. *5 rooms, 1 apartment | tel. 4 37 19 25 and 8 64 13 25 | bjarg@simnet. is | Budget–Moderate*

INSIDER TIP ▶ BORGARNES B&B
Attractive house in central location, close to Englendingavik ('Englishmen's Bay').

Ísafjörður: largest town and traditional commercial centre of the Westfjords

HYRNAN
The eats at this value-for-money grill restaurant at the service station makes it a popular and crowded choice. *Brúartorg | Budget–Moderate*

Well furnished, spacious rooms – a really good deal. Breakfast buffet provided, otherwise guests are free to use the kitchen. *7 rooms | Skulagata 21 | tel. 4 34 15 66 and 8 42 58 66 | www.borgarnesbb.is | Budget*

SPORTS & ACTIVITIES

SÖGUHRINGURINN
Guided walking tour (in English) for groups, hot on the trail of Egill. *June–Aug | Starting at the Landnámssetur Museum (see p. 69) | By arrangement: tel. 4 37 16 00 | 28,000 ISK per group*

INFORMATION

WEST ICELAND TOURIST INFORMATION
In the shopping centre, *Hyrnutorg. Borgarbraut 58–60 | tel. 4 37 22 14 | www.west.is*

WHERE TO STAY

BJARG
Cosy accommodation on a converted farm. Choose between an apartment and double or four-bed rooms with shared bathroom. There's also a cabin with two rooms. Located 1km/0.62mi along Rte. 1

WHERE TO GO

BORG Á MÝRUM (119 D3) (∅ E8)
This site, a little to the north of Borgarnes, is where Skallagrímur Kvéldúlfsson and later Snorri Sturluson built their farmsteads. The sculpture Snorratorrek by Ásmundur Sveinsson represents Egill's lament for the death of his son, Böðvar.

HRAUNFOSSAR (119 F2–3) *(ᗰ F–G7)*
Some 55km/34mi east of Borgarnes, a group of waterfalls, spread over a distance of 1km/0.62mi, cascade from the *Hallmundarhraun* lava field. This INSIDERTIP watery spectacle is particularly stunning in September, when the vegetation glows in its autumnal hues. At 1.6 km/1mi in length, the tunnel-like lava cave *Surtshellir* (119 F2) *(ᗰ G7)* near Húsafell is the largest in the country and was inhabited in the 10th century.

REYKHOLT ★ (119 E3) *(ᗰ F7)*
Today's school and parish centre, 40km/25mi to the east, was once home to Snorri Sturluson. An underground passage linked his former house and his ● *hot pot,* 'Snorralaug', and it was here that he was murdered on 22 September 1241. This stone-walled *bathing pool* is one of the few remaining constructions from the Middle Ages. Snorri and further members of his family lie buried at the *cemetery*. The exhibition at the *Snorrastofa* study centre gives an insight into Snorri's works *(May–Sept daily 10am–6pm, Oct–April Mon–Fri 10am–5pm | Admission: 600 ISK | www.reykholt.is).* There's a programme of classical music concerts in the church every summer.

A good place to stay is the *Fosshotel Reykholt,* offering a high standard of comfort *(53 rooms | tel. 4 35 12 60 | www. fosshotel.is | Moderate–Expensive).*

ÍSAFJÖRÐUR

(112 C2) *(ᗰ C3)* **The fishing industry is the main source of income for the 2900 inhabitants of the largest town in the Westfjords region; it was a major trading centre within the Hanseatic League back in the 16th century.**

Once the Danish trading monopoly had been relaxed in the 18th century, the town really began to flourish. A number of buildings from this era still survive. A *seamen's monument* at the cemetery pays tribute to the fishermen and other seafarers who drowned off the coast. A further hint at the close links to the sea is the *whalebone arch* in the park.

SIGHTSEEING

BYGGÐASAFN VESTFJARÐA – WESTFJORDS FOLK MUSEUM
The museum is housed in a former warehouse dating back to the 18th century and documents not only maritime but also municipal history. *June–Aug Mon–Fri 10am–5pm, Sat/Sun 1pm–5pm | Admission: 550 ISK | Neðstakaupstaður*

FOOD & DRINK

MUSEUM CAFÉ
At lunchtimes, there's a soup of the day, a selection of small snacks and the traditional salted fish. *June–Aug daily 1pm–5pm | Neðstikaupstaður | Budget–Moderate*

★ **Reykholt**
Snorri Sturluson, author and politician, lived here → p. 71

★ **Dynjandi**
Iceland's most beautiful waterfall is close to the coast → p. 72

★ **Látrabjarg**
The country's westernmost cliffs are inhabited by thousands of seabirds → p. 73

★ **Snæfellsjökull National Park**
The famous glacier with the almost magical aura → p. 75

MARCO POLO HIGHLIGHTS

VESTURSTÓÐ

Café and restaurant in a historic and stylishly furnished house. Tasty bistro-style eats. *Aðalstræti 7 | tel. 4 56 66 20 | Budget–Moderate*

SPORTS & ACTIVITIES

VESTURFERÐIR

Excursions around the region, kayak tours, bicycle hire, riding tours. *Aðalstræti 7 | tel. 4 56 51 11 | www.vesturferdir.is*

Iceland's most beautiful waterfall tumbles down into the valley: the Dynjandi

WHERE TO STAY

ÁSLAUGUR GUEST HOUSE

Stay in this conveniently located guest house in a historic building in the centre of town. There's also sleeping-bag accommodation and an apartment in the adjacent building. Guests can use the kitchen. *14 rooms | Austurvegur 7 | tel. 4 56 38 68 | Budget*

HOTEL EDDA ÍSAFJÖRÐUR

Boarding-school-type accommodation, plus space for sleeping-bag fans and a campsite. *40 rooms | Torfnes school | tel. 4 44 49 60 | www.hoteledda.is | Budget–Moderate*

INFORMATION

TOURIST INFORMATION

Aðalstræti 7 | tel. 4 50 80 60 | www.vestfirdir.is

WHERE TO GO

DYNJANDI ★ ● (112 C3–4) (*∅ C4*)

This must be Iceland's prettiest waterfall. Also known as *Fjallfoss*, it lies 80km/50mi to the south of Ísafjörður. The water plunges 100m/328ft in several fan-shaped cascades. Directly below, there are five more waterfalls, each delightful in its own right. The best view of this waterfall panorama is to be had ☀ from the coast. Dynjandi – 'the thundering one' – is part of a protected nature reserve. You'll find a campsite on the coast.

HNJÓTUR (112 A4) (*∅ A4*)

Collector Egill Ólafsson has amassed a hotchpotch of regional artefacts – including aircraft – and displays them at this small museum, 160km/100mi to the south! *June–Sept daily 10am–6pm | Admission: 700 ISK*

HORNSTRANDIR
(112–113 C–D1) (*∭ C–D 1–2*)
The 580km²/224mi² Hornstrandir Peninsula in the far north is a hiker's paradise, where the countless abandoned farmhouses – some of them now being reused as summer holiday cottages – are the only reminder of earlier settlements. Rich vegetation and flocks of seabirds, which nest on the steep cliffs at, for example, INSIDER TIP *Hornbjarg,* are real highlights in the region. Departing from Ísafjörður, the excursions by boat through the nature reserve are a great idea for a day out. Information and tours: *West Tours (tel. 4 56 51 11 | www.vesturferdir.is).*

LÁTRABJARG ★ ☆ (112 A4) (*∭ A4*)
The *Bjargtangar* lighthouse, 180km/120mi from Ísafjörður, marks the westernmost point in Iceland, and therefore Europe. It stands atop the precipitous cliffs of the 14km/8.7mi-long Látrabjarg Peninsula, which, at their highest point, tower more than 440m/1443ft above the sea. ● Thousands of seabirds build their nests on the cliffs; alongside puffins, there is a huge colony of razorbills. A footpath takes you to the picturesque INSIDER TIP *Rauðisandur beach* with its yellowy-red sand. Modest accommodation is to be had in *Breiðavík*, 13 km north of Látrabjarg *(17 rooms | tel. 4 56 15 75 | www.breidavik.is | Budget–Moderate).*

STYKKIS-HÓLMUR

(123 C1) (*∭ C–D6*) **Thanks to its sheltered harbour, Stykkishólmur on the Snæfellsnes Peninsula was one of the Hanseatic League's trading posts in the 16th century, together with Ísafjörður, Rif, Arnarstapi and Flatey.**

A few well preserved old houses still stand close to the harbour. Today's population of 1100 lives mainly from fishing. You can take the 'Baldur' ferry from Stykkishólmur to the south coast of the Westfjords.

SIGHTSEEING

SÚGANDISEY ☆
Island which is joined to the mainland by a causeway, thereby offering protection to the harbour. From here, you have a fine view of the islands scattered across the Breiðafjörður bay.

INSIDER TIP VATNASAFN ●
The Library of Water is an installation by American artist Roni Horn: twenty-four glass tubes filled with water from Iceland's glaciers, their changing, shimmering colours dictated by the incidence of light. *5 May–Aug daily 11am–5pm | Free admission | Bókhlöðustigur 17*

LOW BUDGET

▶ *Venus* is the name of a very pretty campsite near Borgarnes, offering a great view and value-for-money eats at the restaurant in *Mótel Venus (Hafnarskógur | tel. 4 37 23 45 | motel@centrum.is).*

▶ The *Sjónarhóll Youth Hostel* is located in one of the oldest buildings in Stykkishólmur, but the rooms have been renovated and are comfy enough. Mostly dormitory accommodation, with a total of 50 beds. *Höfðagata 1 | tel. 4 38 10 95 and 8 61 25 17 | www.hostel.is*

FOOD & DRINK

FIMM FISKAR
Fish dishes of the first order at the 'Five Fishes' restaurant and a pretty terrace for outdoor diners. *Frúarstígur 1 | tel. 4 36 16 00 | www.simnet.is/fimmfiskar | Moderate*

NARFEYRARSTOFA
There is a cosy *café (Budget)* on the ground floor of this pretty old house. At the *restaurant (Moderate)* on the first floor you should try the fish soup, made with fish from the fjord. *Aðalgata 3 | tel. 4 38 11 19 | www.narfeyrarstofa.is*

SPORTS & ACTIVITIES

The *Tourist Information Centre* offers guided walking tours focusing on the architecture of the old part of town. Boat trips, including the chance to try sea angling, do a bit of birdwatching or catch some mussels, are run by *Seatours (Excursion: 5950 ISK | Smið justígur 3 | tel. 4 38 14 50 | www.seatours.is).*

WHERE TO STAY

ORLOFSIBÚÐIR
Tastefully furnished apartments (65–75m² 700–800ft) in various houses. You're sure of a comfortable stay in this quiet location. Ideal for families. *12 apartments | tel. 8 91 31 23 | www.orlof sibudir.is | Moderate*

STYKKISHÓLMUR ☆
Situated just outside town on a hill, this hotel offers a great view and very comfortable rooms. *79 rooms | Borgarbraut 8 | tel. 4 30 21 00 | www.hringhotels.is | Expensive*

ÞINGVELLIR ☆
This secluded B&B scores with its fabulous views and is a good base for beauti-

THE VIKINGS

Real bad guys, legend has it, who roamed the known world murdering, thieving and pillaging as they went. This image, though, does not tally with that of you're average Icelandic Viking. These were free farmers from Norway who refused to subject themselves to the authority of King Haraldur. Their search for suitable land to settle in brought them to Iceland. Flóki Vilgerðarson set out back in 865 and landed on the north-west coast. He gave the new territory the name Ìsland ('ice land') because he was forced to remain here for two winters, trapped by the ice floes. Despite this hardly flatter-ing designation, word of the land spread quickly, and large-scale settlement began in earnest from 874.

The West was much prized by the settlers for its rich pastureland and plentiful fishing grounds. A number of very rich farmers and 'Goden' (see p. 41), such as Snorri Sturluson, lived here. Some of the best known sagas, too, are set in these parts; *Egil's Saga*, the *Laxdæla Saga* and also the ones about Erik the Red have their origins in this region. It's not surprising, then, that in many places in the West you can come across numerous traces of these saga heroes, the Icelandic Vikings.

ful walks down to the sea. *4 rooms | Access from Rte. 58 | tel. 4 38 10 51 and 8 65 04 24 | www.tingvellir.com | Budget*

TOURIST INFORMATION
In the club house at the golf course. *Aðalgata 29 | tel. 4 33 81 20 | www.stykkisholmur.is*

WHERE TO GO

EIRÍKSSTAÐIR (119 E1) *(𝄞 E6)*
Some 50km/30mi west of Stykkishólmur in the Haukadalur valley at the foot of the Stóra-Vatnshorn lies the birthplace of Leifur Eiríksson. A reconstruction of the longhouse, built by Leifur's father, Erik the Red, in the 10th century, was erected here in 2000. The site gives an impressive insight into life at the time. *June–Aug daily 9am–6pm | Admission: 800 ISK | On Rte. 586 | www.leif.is*

FLATEY (112 C5) *(𝄞 C5)*
Today, the island in the Breiðafjörður is more of a summer stopover, but in the 19th century it was a major cultural centre. 'Flat island' became famous due to the Flateyarbók manuscript from the end of the 14th century, which describes, among other things, Leifur Eiríksson's voyage to America. The quaint village and its handful of old houses share the island with a large breeding ground for seabirds. The 'Baldur' ferry makes for Flatey every day, both from the north-west coast as well as from Stykkishólmur. Information and tickets from *Seatours (see p. 74 | Day trip: 5400 ISK | www.seatours.is)*, which can also organise accommodation on Flatey.

SNÆFELLSJÖKULL NATIONAL PARK ★
(119 A2) *(𝄞 B6–7)*
In the centre of the 167-km²/65mi² National Park between the villages of Hell-

Archetypal sculpture of Leifur Eiríksson in Eiríksstaðir, en route for America

nar in the South and Hellissandur in the North, is the 1446m/4744ft-high volcanic peak, *Snæfellsjökull*. People believe that the mountain and its immediate surroundings generate a special kind of energy. The coast at the foot of the volcano is particularly fascinating. Far to the south, the rock pillars at *Lóndrangar,* presumably once magma vents, tower up out of the sea, and out to the west is *Dritvík* on the bay of the same name, an important fishing port until the 19th century. All that remains of this once busy settlement are a few ruined buildings and four INSIDER TIP lifting stones of various weights – whoever was not able to lift 49 kg, was not allowed to sign on as a fisherman!

Glacier tours on snowcats start from Arnarstapi *(Snjófell | Arnarstapi | tel. 4 35 67 83 | www.snjofell.is)*. You can book a guided hike through the National Park *(Hotel Hellissandur | Hellissandur | tel. 4 30 86 00 | www.hotelhellissandur.is)*. Information about the National Park is available from the *Information Centre (Hellnar | tel. 4 36 68 88 | www.ust.is)*.

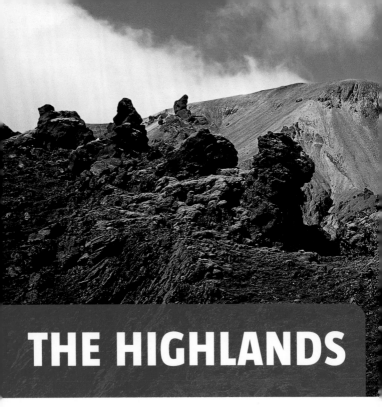

THE HIGHLANDS

The uninhabited Highland region is Iceland at its most primal and breathtaking, a landscape fashioned by volcanic activity and ice. The Hofsjökull and Langjökull glaciers and monumental table mountains, such as the Herðubreið, tower into the sky from the grey-brown lava and gravel plains, dotted with colourful patches of vegetation.

Depending on the weather, the bizarre lava formations seem metamorphosed into menacing figures. For centuries, the two highland routes *Sprengisandsleið* and *Kjalvegur* were the main connection between the North and South, but every traveller was relieved to finally reach his home farm again. The other highland roads were also cross-country riding trails. In the Middle Ages, as a matter of fact, there were also routes across the Vatnajökull glacier – the shortest links between the different regions. These rides, however, were not without their dangers, since numerous outlaws had retreated into the inhospitable Highlands and survived by means of highway robbery. The name of the huge, forbidding lava desert *Ódáðahraun* – which means something like 'Evil Deeds Lava' – hints at this fact. Trolls and giants are said to inhabit the region, too ...

Today, the rivers and lava fields of the Highlands are a challenge for off-road drivers, mountain bikers and hikers. Almost all trails are well marked, there are a number of mountain huts and campsites, but self-sufficiency is the norm here.

Photo: At the Brennisteinsalda crater near Landmannalaugar

Deserts, mountains and glaciers:
in total silence through the lonely wilderness
– a world away from civilisation

FJALLABAK-
SLEIÐ NYRÐI

The 'northern trail behind the mountains' runs from west to east and was an essential link for centuries.

The roughly 84km/52mi-long route (Rte. F 208) begins in the north-west near the Sigalda power plant on the *Hrauneyalón lake* (120 C3) *(ᗺ J9)* and ends in the south-east near *Búland* (121 D5) *(ᗺ K11)*, where it joins Rte. 208. It may be a more interesting option to follow the *Land-mannaleið* (Rte. F 225) which runs southwards for the first 47km/30mi before intersecting with Rte. F 208 at the *Frost-aðavatn lake* (120 C4) *(ᗺ J10)*. The trail climbs in some places to heights of between 500 and 1000 m (1650 and 3300ft) and leads through a bizarre, yet beautiful, landscape. To the north of the Hekla volcano, the *Sölvahraun* lava field, with its crevasses and craters, cloaked in black ash, presents an apocalyptic picture.

Popular 'bathtub' for a chat and a soak: the Landmannalaugar warm springs

To the east of the lava fields around Hekla is Iceland's largest area of rhyolite deposits, covering around 400km²/155mi². Rhyolite is a siliceous volcanic rock, notable for its reddish or greenish colour.

SIGHTSEEING

ELDGJÁ (121 D4) (🗺 K10)
The 'Fire Gorge', in English, extends for over 40km/25mi from the Uxatíndar peak as far as the edge of the Mýrdalsjökull glacier in the south-west and looks particularly breathtaking near ⚇ Gjátindur (935m/3067ft) where it is 5km/3.1mi long, over 200m/656ft deep and up to 600m/1970ft wide. The south-westerly section of the Eldgjá rift consists of a row of craters. Some of their lava flows reached as far as the Mýrdalssandur sandar plain in South Iceland, around 5000 years ago. The impressive north-eastern section was formed by an eruption as late as the 10th century.

LANDMANNALAUGAR ⭐
(120 C4) (🗺 J10)
In the 'people's warm springs', the farmers of past centuries used to recuperate from the arduous task of driving their sheep back down the mountains for the winter. Today, they are possibly Iceland's best known 'bathtub', surrounded by multi-coloured rhyolite peaks. From ⚇ Bláhnúkur (943m/3093ft) – which gets its name from its blue-green shimmering rock – you can look across to the vast obsidian lava field Laugahraun, a labyrinthine expanse of black lava formations, some up to 40m/131ft high.

WHERE TO STAY

LANDMANNALAUGAR HUT
Der Icelandic *Touring Association (Fí)* runs a large mountain hut with a warden and space for up to 78 overnight visitors *(Budget)*. Advance booking is essential. There's also a large campsite.

From here, the Fí also offers a four-day hike to Þórsmörk along the famous *Laugavegur* trail. *Ferðafélags Íslands (Fí) | Mörkin 6 | Reykjavík | tel. 5 68 25 33 and 8 60 33 35 (in summer) | www.fi.is*

KALDIDALUR

Route F 550, ☆ the Kaldidalsvegur Route (119 F3) *(∅ F–G 7–8)***, is only 40km/25mi long and runs from Húsafell as far as Rte. 52 near Þingvellir, past the two glaciers, Langjökull and Þórisjökull in the East and the 1198m/3930ft-high glacial peak, Ok, in the West.**

The Kaldidalur owes its name, 'cold valley', to this geographical constellation, climbing as it does to around 700m/2300ft in some places. The real beauty of the trail lies in the views of the glaciers combined with the sight of a number of landmark peaks, such as *Prestahnúkur* (1069m/3507ft) which consists of greenish rhyolite rock.

The final destination, *Húsafell,* is one of the Icelanders' favourite places to head for at weekends. Its plentiful coverage of trees and a host of hiking paths mean the area has many weekend cottages and also a large campsite. In the more distant past, the original Húsafell farmstead was an important supply point for travellers on route from North to South. From here, you can undertake excursions to the Langjökull and to the large lava caves, *Surtshellir* and *Stefánshellir* (119 F2) *(∅ G7)* in the Hallmundarhraun lava field, located to the north of the village on Rte. 518. The trail leading there is passable by car; the route is signposted and car parking is available.

KJALVEGUR

The imposing highland route, Kjalvegur (Rte. F 35), leads from Gullfoss in the South (120 B2–3) *(∅ H9)* **165km/102mi northwards to the Blanda power plant above the Blöndulón lake** (114 B4) *(∅ H6)*.

Probably the most impressive section of the journey runs through the *Kjölur* valley, a deserted lava and gravel plain at an altitude of almost 700m/2300ft between the Langjökull and Hofsjökull glaciers. The trail originally ran further west through the Kjalhraun, but it was re-routed in the wake of a tragic accident in 1780. Four people, together with 180 sheep and 16 horses, died here in a snow storm. To this day, the INSIDER TIP *Beinahóll hill* is strewn with animal bones. In this vast expanse of desert terrain, there is no shelter against wind and weather for miles.

★ **Landmannalaugar**
Warm springs surrounded by multi-coloured rhyolite peaks → p. 78

★ **Hveravellir**
An oasis for travellers: the thermal area in the middle of the Kjölur valley → p. 80

★ **Askja**
Iceland's second-deepest lake, the Öskjuvatn, lies in a stunning caldera → p. 81

★ **Kverkfjöll**
Fire and ice – you can't get more Icelandic than this → p. 82

MARCO POLO HIGHLIGHTS

SIGHTSEEING

HVERAVELLIR ⭐ (114 C6) (*⬚ J7*)

Halfway along the Kjölur, and on the northern edge of the Kjalhraun, lies the thermal area of Hveravellir and its bubbling, seething springs and solfataras. Travellers back in the Middle Ages appreciated a dip in the warm waters; the hot springs were used for cooking. There are around 20 springs; some of them are stunningly beautiful. *Bláhver*, the 7m/23ft-wide 'Blue Pool', is characterised by sinter deposits and brimming with turquoise-to-aquamarine blue water. The ultimate picture-postcard image is surely *Fagrihver*, the 'Beautiful Pool', with its clear, shimmering turquoise waters.

In the 18th century, the outlaw Fjalla Eyvindur and his wife hid on the *Kjalhraun* lava field. The INSIDER TIP lava cave – their hideout in the Highland region for 20 years – can still be seen.

INSIDER TIP KERLINGARFJÖLL (120 C1) (*⬚ J8*)

The myriad colours of the rhyolite mountain ranges towering over the Kjölur plain are visible for miles around. ↘ The highest peaks, Snækollur (1477m/4846ft), Loðmundur (1432m/4698ft) and Mænir (1355m/4445ft) are partially covered with ice caps. The laborious ascent is rewarded with a view reaching from South to North of the island. In some of the multi-coloured, glistening valleys, solfataras make for a steaming, spluttering spectacle. This is the place to experience Iceland in miniature: fire and ice in close proximity. The Kerlingarfjöll range is perfect hiking country.

SPORTS & ACTIVITIES

A very enjoyable three-day hike takes you along the Langjökull and parallel to the old Kjalvegur as far as the glacial lake Hvítárvatn and on to Hveravellir. *Book via Fí (see p. 79)*

WHERE TO STAY

HVERAVELLIR (114 C6) (*⬚ J7*)

Two mountain huts, open all year round, for up to 53 people in sleeping-bag accommodation and bunks. There's also a campsite. Broad range of tours on offer and a natural pool. Bookings: *www.hveravellir.is* | *Budget*

KERLINGARFJÖLL (120 C1) (*⬚ J8*)

There is accommodation for 28 in the main building, plus twelve cabins sleeping between five and twelve. Well-equipped

SUPER JEEPS

Four-wheel vehicles in Iceland are real eye-catchers; with their 44-inch tyres and correspondingly modified, wide bodywork, they look rather intimidating. But when you drive along one of the highland trails yourself, you'll wish you could trade your vehicle for one of these super jeeps. They positively glide over lava, stones and all uneven surfaces. In winter, in particular, their strengths come to the fore, as their thick tyres effortlessly negotiate the snowy surface. These tyres can even be driven at a pressure of 0.1 bar. Consequently, such off-road jeeps are used by rescue services and the fire brigade.

campsite. There's a restaurant and a whirl-pool to relax in. *Tel. 664 78 78 (in summer)* | *www.kerlingarfjoll.is* | *Budget*

ÖSKJULEIÐ

The way to Heaven leads through Hell, so they say: you could certainly say this of this trail (F 88).

It leads through ● INSIDERTIP *Ódáðahraun*, Iceland's largest expanse of lava wasteland,

SIGHTSEEING

ASKJA ⭐ **(122 A1)** *(ጠ N6)*

In the heart of the Dyngjufjöll range, a typical central volcanic system which has been active for hundreds of thousands of years, lies a true natural monument: the Askja caldera with its dazzlingly blue lake, Öskjuvatn. The crater was formed around 6000 years ago and is almost circular, measuring 8km/5mi in diameter. Its sides are between 200 and 400 m (655

Panoramic views of the Highlands open up from the campsite at Hveravellir

covering an area of 4500 km²/1737mi² (116 A–B 4–6, 122 A–B 1–2) *(ጠ M–O 4–7)*. Lava dating back 5000 years, sand, gravel and a number of monolithic, looming table mountains of palagonite give it its distinctive appearance: black and menacing, dismal and arid. Rainfall seeps away so quickly through the loose, porous stone – volcanic in origin – that plants are unable to make use of the moisture. Only at the edges of the lava desert, where the ground water escapes through small springs, can green and fruitful oases such as *Herðu-breiðarlindir* evolve. The Öskjuleið trail leads over 88km/55mi through this wilderness as far as the northern edge of the Vatnajökull and the famous Askja caldera.

and 1310ft) high and are precipitously steep in places.

The best view of the Askja is to be had from 🌿 *Þorvaldstindur* (1510m/4955ft) on the southern edge of Dyngjufjöll. The *Öskjuvatn* lake, 217m/711ft deep, was the result of a massive eruption in 1875. At the time, a cloak of ash buried 16 farms and 10,000 km²/3860mi² of land. In 1907, German geologist Walther von Knebel and his compatriot Max Rudolff, a painter, disappeared without a trace during an exploratory trip on the lake. On the northern edge of Öskjuvatn lies the crater lake *Víti* with its milky, green-blue water. The last eruption to take place in the Dyngjufjöll was in 1961.

Angelica and willowherb in front of the cloud-covered Herðubreið

HERÐUBREIÐARLINDIR
(116 B6) (*∅ O6*)

Lush greenery and over 100 species of plant can be marvelled at in this oasis which is fed by the waters of the river Lindaá and forms part of the *Herðubreiðarfriðland* National Park. A particularly striking feature is the abundance of angelica growing here and, after the silence of the lava wastelands, the vibrant sound of birdsong is not to be overheard. Some 30 species, most commonly the snow bunting, thrive here among the many plants and insects. Herðubreiðarlindir takes its name from the formidable 🔆 *Herðubreið* mountain (1682m/ 5518ft), formed during an eruption under the 1000m/3280ft-thick ice crust during the last Ice Age. The ascent is difficult due to the loose covering of scree underfoot, but the view from the top is overwhelming.

WHERE TO STAY

DREKI HUT ON DYNGJUFJÖLL
(122 A1) (*∅ N6*)

The mountain hut sleeps 55 visitors and is run by Akureyri Touring Club. There is a warden on site and also a campsite. *FFA | Strandgata 23 | Akureyri | tel. 4 62 27 20 and 8 22 51 90 | www.ffa.is | Budget*

ÞORSTEINSSKÁLI HUT
(122 B1) (*∅ N6*)

The hut, with a resident warden, has room for 30 overnight guests. You will find also an attractive campsite nearby. *FFA (see above | tel. 8 22 51 91)*

WHERE TO GO

KVERKFJÖLL ⭐
(122 A3) (*∅ N8*)

The mountain range on the northern edge of the Vatnajökull, 45km/28mi south of the Askja, is a volcanic system with an ice-filled caldera. The glacier tongue *Kverkjökull* pushes its way out of a north-facing opening. One of Iceland's largest geothermal areas lies on the western flank of the range: *Hveradalur.* Here, a series of fascinating ice caves and tunnels have been carved out underneath the glacier.

SPRENGI-SANDSLEIÐ

The 250km/155mi-long Sprengisand-sleið Route (F 26) runs from the Mýri farm in the North (115 F4) *(𝄞 M5)* **down to the Þjórsárdalur valley in the South** (120 B–C3) *(𝄞 H–J9).*

The trail passes through the *Sprengisan-dur*, Iceland's largest stone desert, stretch-ing from the Hofsjökull to the Tung-nafellsjökull glaciers and measuring over 70km/43mi from north to south. The name, which also designates the route, only came into use in the 18th century. In the Middle Ages, it was simply known as Sandur (sand). The tacked-on word *spren-gir* derives from the verb sprengja (to tire out). Sprengisandur was not only feared because of its sandstorms and highway-men, but also because the individual grazing grounds were more than a day's ride apart. Not surprisingly, riders were keen to reach their destination by night-fall and correspondingly rode many a horse to death in the process.

SIGHTSEEING

HOFSJÖKULL
(114–115 C–D6) *(𝄞 J–K7)*
The third-largest glacier in the country covers an area of 995 km²/384mi². Its white cap can be seen from miles away and measures up to 1760m/5774ft high. It may appear peaceful, but below the summit a giant volcano slumbers. On the south-east periphery of the glacier is the *Þjórsárver* Nature Reserve, a swampy area with typical moorland vegetation, lakes and ponds. It is the favourite breed-ing area of the pink-footed goose; around 11,000 pairs nest and rear their young here.

NÝIDALUR (121 E1) *(𝄞 L7)*
This valley on the southern side of the Tungnafellsjökull glacier lies at an alti-tude of over 800m/2625ft and is sur-prisingly green – probably the highest point in the country to boast flowering meadows. The tourist hut in the south of the valley is an ideal starting point for hikes in the surrounding area, for exam-ple, to the geothermal area south of the Tungnafellsjökull on the *Eggja* mountain (1271m/4170ft).

WHERE TO STAY

NÝIDALUR (121 E1) *(𝄞 L7)*
The *Icelandic Touring Association (Fí)* owns two huts *(Budget)*, offering accom-modation for 120 people. From the 🌿 green plain, you have a great view of the glacier. There is also a pleasant campsite close by. *Book via Fí (see p. 79)*

LOW BUDGET

▶ Armed with backpack, tent, good hiking maps and several days' ra-tions, your 'Hiking in the Highlands' adventure can begin. Deserted land-scapes, challenging trails, rivers to wade through – nature at its finest. Countless mountains are just waiting to be climbed, glaciers to be crossed. Some campsites are free.

▶ For the more daring of you, go for a dip in 'Hell', as Víti translates into English. Blissfully warm water, but stinking to high heaven of sulphur! There's no shower or changing room – after all, Hell doesn't afford any luxury either.

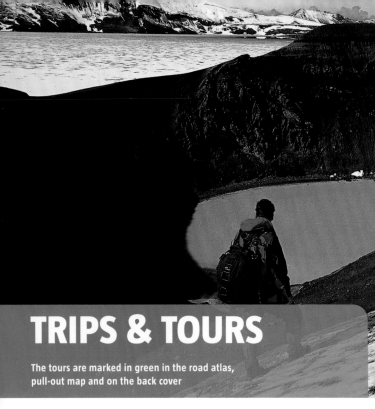

TRIPS & TOURS

The tours are marked in green in the road atlas,
pull-out map and on the back cover

1 NATURE & CULTURE: THE GOLDEN CIRCLE

The Golden Circle is without doubt the most popular tour in Iceland; plenty of travel companies in the country offer this package, but you can also drive it yourself as almost all the roads are asphalted. On the way, you pass Halldór Laxness's house, visit the Icelanders' national shrine, þingvellir, and experience the forces of nature in the form of the geysers, Geysir and Strokkur, and the Gullfoss waterfall. On the return journey, make a detour to Skálholt, bishop's seat and cultural centre from 1056 to 1785. To really enjoy the sights along the 220km/135mi-long route, you should set aside two days and take along plenty to eat and drink.

The tour includes the best known natural and cultural monuments, a kind of 'Best of' selection for every Iceland visitor, even those only staying in the country for a few days. Take Rte. 1 from Reykjavík → p. 32 heading north to Mosfellsbær, 9km/5.6mi away. Just before you leave the village, Rte. 36 branches off to the right, taking you in the direction of Þingvellir. After a few kilometres, you come to Laxness Farm, where the Nobel prize-winner spent his childhood and from which he later took his name. Close by, to the right, you can see his house, 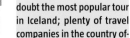 INSIDER TIP Gljufrasteinn, where he lived with his family from 1945 onwards. The building has many a story to tell and is

Photo: Askja with the Viti crater and its lake

Cultural monuments and highland thrills: trips to glaciers and geysers, deserts and waterfalls

now a museum *(daily 10am–5pm | 800 ISK | www.gljufrasteinn.is)*.

When you are up on the Mosfellsheiði plain, you'll be able to see Iceland's largest lake, Þingvallavatn, and the adjoining National Park, Þingvellir → p. 40. After around 30km/18mi, your route takes you to the right and to the Information Centre and ☀️ observation point. From here, you can see far into the Highlands. Either you now start your walk through the National Park or you continue along Rte. 36 as far as its junction

with Rte. 362. A number of marked footpaths lead from the car parks to the Lögberg, to the Öxaráfoss waterfall and to the Almannagjá.

Back on Rte. 36, then turn onto Rte. 365 after approximately 8km/5mi towards Laugarvatn. The 16km/10mi-long stretch of road leads through an attractive lava landscape, the foothills of an extinct shield volcano. The woods around the village of Laugarvatn make this a popular choice for a day out during the summer months, and there are a number of holiday cottages in the area. Besides that, Laugarvatn is a centre of education, with the district boarding school, a domestic science college and a sports college. The hot springs are used largely to heat greenhouses. The *Hótel Edda – ML Laugarvatn (99 rooms | tel. 4 44 40 00 and 4 44 48 10 | www.hoteledda.is | Budget–Moderate)*, located close to the lake and the steam bath, has a homely feel, despite its size. *Tourist Information Office at the campsite (tel. 4 86 11 55)*

Heading north-east first of all on Rte. 37 and then continuing on Rte. 35 takes you to Geysir in Haukadalur – from a distance you can already pick out the plume from the **Strokkur** geyser. Its hotel, campsite and attractive hiking trails make **Geysir** → p. 49 a good choice for a longer stay. The impressive **Gullfoss** → p. 50 waterfall is just 7km/4.4mi further on.

The return journey is via Rte. 35, past the small village of **Reykholt**, conspicuous by its many greenhouses. The warm springs are typical of this region and are mainly used for agricultural purposes. Furthermore, this is a favourite place for a weekend getaway, with good angling rivers. Some 25km/15mi from Gullfoss, you reach Rte. 31 which brings you back to the bishopric of **Skálholt** → p. 50. Here, it's worth taking a look at the church and then walking out to the relatively extensive excavations and the reconstructed farmstead.

Back on Rte. 35, your route takes you southwards. After 18km/11mi, the 3000-year-old explosion crater **Kerið** appears on the left, 55m/180ft deep and with a lake at its base. Shortly before you join the Ring Road to Reykjavík, you come past **Fjallstún** at the foot of the Ingólfsfjall, supposedly the site where the first settler, Ingólfur Arnarson, spent the winter on the island. From the junction it's around 50km/30mi to Reykjavík, where a break at **Hveragerði** → p. 45 will get your strength back.

Lush, summer grass at the foot of the Langjökull glacier

2 SKIRTING THE GLACIER: KJALVEGUR

A great hike – ideal even for beginners – covering around 50km/30mi. Set aside around four days to tackle it. The individual stages are relatively short, without significant differences in altitude and are well signposted. You'll be walking at the foot of the second-biggest glacier in Iceland, the Langjökull, amidst a most varied lava landscape. You can stay the night in mountain huts, but tent, sleeping bag, sufficient rations and good, waterproof clothing and shoes are an absolute must. In addition, you'll need an up-to-date hiking map. During the summer months, buses leave Reykjavík and Akureyri daily via the Kjölur Route. Tell the driver when you get on board that you want to get off at Hvítárnes.

On day one, you follow the 8km/5mi trail as far as the Hvítárnes hut by the Hvítárvatn lake on Langjökull's eastern edge. Here, the Nyrðriskriðjökull glacier calves into the lake which is scattered with small, floating icebergs. The red-roofed hut was constructed in 1930, and the ruins of a farm can be seen directly next to it. It is assumed that settlers made the area their home back in the 9th century, as the lake had a good stock of fish.

On the second day, walk the 12km/7.5mi as far as the Þverbrekknamúli hut. First of all, orientate yourself by following the stone cairns to the east of the hut which mark the old Kjalvegur → p. 79 route. Then follow the clearly recognisable footpath north-eastwards along the Fúlakvísl river. The table mountain, Hrútfell (1410m/462ft), is an impressive sight in the distance, and to the east you'll notice the Kerlingarfjöll → p. 80 range. Once you have crossed the Þverbrekknaver

marsh, a bridge takes you over the river, and the way to the hut is marked by posts. Þverbrekknamúli is a good starting point for ⚞ mountain hikes on Hrútfell or to the Fjallkirkja rock formation 15 km/9mi away on the Langjökull. This is the site of the INSIDER TIP *Kirkjuból* hut, owned by the Icelandic Glacier Research Society.

The third day's hike is 15km/9mi long. Return to the bridge and continue along the old Kjalvegur Route. Since you will not be crossing any further rivers, you should take water with you from the streams at the hut. Initially, the trail runs parallel to the Fúlakvísl, which winds through a narrow gorge. Further on, you should head northwards, towards the Þjófafell (960m/3150ft) peak. You now come to the green banks of the Þjófadalaá. Follow this stream into the Þjófadalir valley, west of the mountain, and as far as the next hut. This sheltered valley was once a favourite hideout for robbers and highwaymen, hence its name 'Valley of Thieves'. From here you can set off on hikes up ⚞ Rauðkollur (1060ftm/3477) or to the Strýtur crater.

The final 12km/7.5mi lie ahead of you on day four. First, climb the Þröskuldur pass where you meet up with the jeep trail to Hveravellir, the simplest option now being to follow it. In Hveravellir → p. 80, you can recover from the stresses and strains of the tour by taking a dip in the thermal waters, though there are also showers available at the well-equipped campsite and hut.

3 CAPTIVATING WASTELAND: ÖSKJULEIÐ

This is one of Iceland's most beautiful highland routes, through the black and grey wilderness of the lava desert Ódáðahraun, which is dominated by the

'Queen of Mountains', the table mountain Herðubreið. On the way, you'll come across green oases, discover one of the most impressive natural monuments in Iceland, Askja, and delve into the world of the ice caves. For the approximately 300km/186mi journey you should plan three days. This highland trail is only for practised off-road drivers who have experience of driving through rivers. If you have never driven a four-wheel-drive vehicle before, you're better off taking the ● bus, to enable you to enjoy a stress-free tour of the imposing lava landscape. The bus leaves both from Akureyri as well as from Mývatn lake. During the three-day trip (offered between 5 July and 16 August) you sleep in the Sigurðurskáli hut in the Kverkfjöll range, Bring your own food and drink with you. Price: 33,500 ISK, *www.sba.is*. The jeep trail F 88 begins around 40km/25mi east of Mývatn → p. 64. First of all, you come past the Hrossaborg crater, whose partially collapsed rim towers up 40m/130ft. You then drive parallel to the glacial river Jökulsá á Fjöllum, which emerges from the Vatnajökull glacier and plunges further north into the deep in the guise of the mighty Dettifoss → p. 65 waterfall. Unfortunately you only get a few glimpses of it on this trip.

The first ford leads through the Grafarlandaá, and this marks the beginning of the nature reserve which extends over an area of 170km²/65mi² as far as Herðubreiðarlindir → p. 82. Before you reach this pretty oasis, with its bubbling streams and rich vegetation, you have to drive through the Lindaá river as well. It's worth taking a stroll across the nearby field of ropy lava, formed when a thin layer of low-gas-content lava is shoved together by more viscous layers underneath.

The journey continues past an 8km/5mi-long tuff ridge to the south of the Herðu-breið mountain: the 1059m/3474ft-high Herðubreiðartögl. The ground here consists largely of pale pumice formations, whose ash is carried hundreds of kilometres on the stormy winds.

The next destination is the Dyngjufjöll volcano range, its peaks rising 600–700m (1970–2300ft) above the surrounding area, and its caldera, Askja → p. 81. In the centre of the caldera is the Öskjuvatn lake and on its northern edge, the explosion crater, Víti. Despite the sulphurous odour, many visitors like to take a dip in the warm, milky waters of the crater lake. Don't miss a walk into the Drekagil gorge with its bizarre lava formations resembling dragons' heads. The entrance to the gorge lies behind the Dreki mountain hut, to the north-east of the Dyngjufjöll range. To get to the Sigurðurskáli hut, you have to go back 20km/12.5mi and follow the F 910 eastwards. Shortly after the bridge over the Jökulsá á Fjöllum, a trail leads to the south, the F 902. From a distance, you can spot the Kverkfjöll → p. 82, rising up 1929m/6329ft between the two valley glaciers, Dyngjujökull to the west and Brúarjökull to the east. The ice caves, formed on the edge of the glacier by the activity of hot springs, are a fascinating feature. A clearly distinguishable path leads from the hut along the eastern edge of the Kverkjökull glacier tongue to an altitude of ☀ 1840m/6037ft. From here, you have a panoramic view of the Highlands.

The return journey takes you via the F 903 further to the east, which you reach after around 15km/9mi. This takes you to another oasis, Hvannalindir, where you cross the Kreppa and after another 10km/6.2mi re-join the F 910 heading northwards. It's now around 60km/37mi to the Ring Road. Once you have passed both peaks of the Arnardalsfjöll, the F 910 turns to the east, and you continue on the F 905 until you reach ☼ **Möðrudalur**, the highest farm in Iceland. Here you can stop for a rest at the café and enjoy the view towards the Herðubreið and Kverkfjöll mountains. Until just a few years ago, the Ring Road came this way; it has since been re-routed to the north. Following the old road and then continuing along the Ring Road, the return trip to **Akureyri → p. 60** takes you past the attractive Mývatn region.

4 HIKING ON ESJA

Esja stands 914m/2998ft high and, although it is part of the mountain range on the Hvalfjörður fjord, you'd think it was a part of Reykjavík; in fact many residents of the capital actually refer to it as 'their' mountain. Its colour appears to change, depending on the weather. Despite the distance from the city, the importance of the massif for Reykjavík is not to be underestimated, since it protects the city in winter from the strong north-westerly winds. What could make more sense than to climb the 'mountain next door' and take a look at the city from above?

The starting point of this hike, 25km/15.5mi from the city, is the car park at **Mógilsá**. To get there, either drive by car or take the bus. Route no. 15 to Mosfellsbær runs several times a day from Reykjavík. Get off at Háholt and change to the no. 27 to Akranes as far as Mógilsá. The ascent is not difficult – provided you're wearing suitable footwear. There are a number of well signposted paths to the summit, and the climb usually takes around 90 minutes. You'll get a fantastic view from ● ☼ **Þverfellshorn**. In fine weather, you can see across the wide Faxaflói bay and over to the stately outline of Snæfellsjökull.

What also strikes you is the expanse covered by the mini capital, Reykjavík. From Þverfellshorn you can then go on up to the highest point, **Habunga**.

It is also possible to take part in a guided tour: *Arctic Adventures (*price: 9990 ISK | *Laugavegur 11 | tel. 5 62 70 00 | www.adventures.is).*

Dazzling blue ice in a crevasse of the Brúarjökull glacier

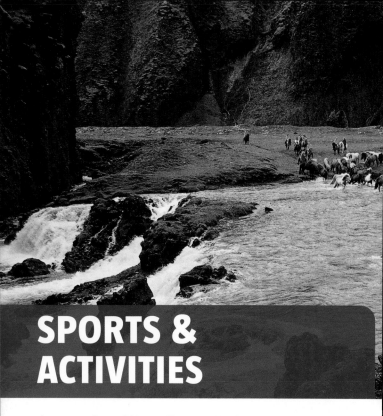

SPORTS & ACTIVITIES

The many outdoor activities on offer are an ideal way to get to know and appreciate Iceland's countryside. The classic way of getting around is riding, and the range of opportunities to ride is consequently huge. Icelanders, however, regard the Icelandic horses more as a means of transport than a piece of sports equipment.

Swimming is a national institution and an essential skill for children to learn. In recent years, hiking and golf have been discovered by an ever-wider audience.

advice from local hiking guides, too. If you are attempting such a tour for the first time, the excursions offered by the Icelandic touring associations are an ideal alternative. Instead, you could also opt for a ride in a jeep or on a snowmobile across the glaciers, as offered by tour operators in Reykjavík and Höfn. A good source of information and operator of tours – especially on the Vatnajökull – are the *Icelandic Mountain Guides (Reykjavík | Vagnhöfði 7b | tel. 5 87 99 99 | www.mountainguides.is)*

GLACIER TOURS

Experienced ice climbers can undertake solo tours across the Langjökull or the Vatnajökull, but it is still important to get

GOLF

There are 65 golf courses in the country, and some greens have been intriguingly incorporated into the lava landscape. Most

Photo: Riders in the Fjallabak nature reserve

In the water or on land, on glaciers or at the lakes: there's a host of things to do in the great Icelandic outdoors

courses are open to foreign visitors for a reasonable green fee. You could even take part in the annual international 'Arctic Open', staged by the Golf Club at Akureyri at the end of June. The tournament begins shortly before midnight and lasts until well into the following morning. Information and registration: *Golfclub Akureyri (tel. 4 62 29 74 | www.arcticopen.is)*

HIKING

The Highlands and the north-west and north-east of Iceland offer hikers solitude and some intense encounters with nature. Some of the trails are well marked and very popular; others you can discover under your own steam. The main prerequisite for a multiday trek is good physical shape and the right equipment, as you must reckon on experiencing all kinds of weather. Good hiking maps and guides for the most popular routes are available from most bookshops in Reykjavík and from the map specialist, Ferðakort *(www. ferdakort.is)*. One-day walks, e.g. on

Hekla or around Skaftafell, are also a great way to see the countryside. To make the most of the experience, though, you need to be prepared to cope with the extremely changeable weather and have suitable clothing, footwear and sufficient provisions. Organised tours of varying degrees of difficulty are offered by the two Icelandic *touring associations* (see 'Mountaineering') and *Icelandic Mountain Guides* in Reykjavík (see 'Glacier Tours').

HORSE RIDING

Horses are synonymous with Iceland, so it's not surprising that there are many opportunities for riding them. These range from one-hour rides – also for complete beginners – to highland tours lasting several weeks, with two horses per rider. The programme offered by *Íshestar* in *Hafnarfjörður* includes short horseback excursions *(tel. 555 70 00 | www.ishestar.is)*. Arinbjörn Jóhannsson at INSIDER TIP Brekkulækur farm will help you get to know the Arnarvatnsheiði plateau; its many lakes make this a beautiful place to hike and watch birds, so Jóhannsson also offers these activities, too *(Brekkulækur | tel. 451 29 38 | www.abbi-island. is)*. Information on other farms offering riding activities is listed in the brochure 'The Ideal Holiday' *(www.farmholidays.is)* and at *www.visiticeland.com*. Personal riding equipment must be disinfected before entering the country!

MARATHON

The oldest marathon in Iceland, featuring international competitors, is the Reykjavík Marathon which takes place every year in the second half of August (on the same day as Culture Night). Instead of the classic 42.2km/26.2mi, you can also opt to run a shorter stretch. The Midnight Run starts at the end of June every year at 10pm. The longest distance is 10km/6.2mi and takes you through Reykjavík. Information, maps of the courses and registration: *www.marathon.is*

MOUNTAIN BIKING

If you couldn't fit your mountain bike in your suitcase, you can hire one in Reykjavík and in a number of other towns and villages. The routes along the coast near Reykjavík or around the Mývatn lake are beautiful and ideal for hobby cyclists. Tourist information offices have lists of places to hire mountain bikes and book guided tours. Information: *Icelandic Mountain Bike Club (www.fjallahjolaklubburinn.is)*

MOUNTAINEERING

The many mountains are an open invitation to climbing enthusiasts, but the prevalence of loose surface rock and the sudden changes in the weather mean that individual tours are only to be recommended for experienced mountaineers. Essential equipment on any mountain excursion should include emergency rations and first-aid kit, plus a bivouac sack and emergency foil blanket. The Icelandic touring associations also offer guided tours. Both have their headquarters in Reykjavík: *Ferðafélag Íslands (Mörkin 6 | tel. 568 25 33 | www.fi.is)*; *Útivist (Laugavegur 178 | tel. 562 10 00 | www.utivist.is)*.

RAFTING

Fun for all the family is to be had at several locations on the larger glacial rivers. Operators include, for example, *Arctic Rafting (Reykjavík | Laugavegur 11 | tel. 562 70 00 | www.arcticrafting.is)* in the South and, in the North in *Varmahlíð*, *Activity Tours (tel. 453 83 83 | www.rafting.is)*

Adventure in the saddle: mountain bikers on the Kjölur Route

SEA ANGLING & FISHING

Iceland's rivers are renowned for their stocks of salmon and trout. The main salmon-fishing season is from mid-June to mid-September – get your application for a fishing licence in early! The trout season varies and depends on the waters in question. Peak time: April/May to September/October. Fishing licences for trout can be obtained at short notice on site, and many farms also offer opportunities to fish. Sea angling is possible from the end of May to the end of August; you can find out about trips and equipment hire from the local tourist information offices in the coastal towns and villages. For salmon licences and further information, contact the *Federation of Icelandic River Owners (Reykjavík | Bændahöllinni, Hagatorgi | tel. 5 53 15 10 | www.angling. is)* or the *Angelclub Lax-á (Kópavogur | Akurhvarf 16 | tel. 5 57 61 00 | www.lax-a. net)*. Equipment brought from outside the country must be disinfected before entering Iceland!

SWIMMING

Swimming is the national sport in Iceland and an important school subject. Once you've tried the warm waters of the open-air swimming pools, you're sure to be hooked. In Reykjavík alone there are seven pools, and several more in the surrounding villages. Here in particular, efforts have been made to upgrade facilities, a fact which makes these the ideal spot for a family day out. Every large town or village has an open-air swimming pool.

WINTER SPORT

In winter, both cross-country and downhill skiing are possible. There are ski resorts at, for example, *Bláfjöll* south of Reykjavík or above Akureyri on *Hlíðarfjall*. Snow conditions permitting, you can undertake attractive cross-country tours all over the island; the Icelanders' favourite areas are the INSIDER TIP north-west and the Mývatn area. In addition, you could try one of the Ski-Doo snowmobile tours on signposted routes.

TRAVEL
WITH KIDS

Icelanders have a decidedly relaxed and uncomplicated attitude towards children. Families are very close-knit; looking after the children is a task shared by all members, and kids, parents and grandparents generally never live far away from each other.

The number of young mothers is comparatively high. Organised child-care is available for children from the age of 18 months, so women have no problems when they decide to go back to work. One-parent families are not discriminated against, but are actively supported by the state.

During the summer months, when it seems life takes place exclusively outdoors, children play out until midnight. School playgrounds, gardens, roads and beaches are their stomping grounds. Icelandic children are brought up to be independent from an early age, and many teenagers work in shops in the afternoons after school. Since Icelanders are keen consumers, it is natural to want to go to work and earn money as soon as possible.

This orientation towards the family is also evident in pricing. Children under 4 years of age pay nothing and the under-12s generally only half-price; this applies both to public transport fares as well as admission charges.

When touring with children, it's a good idea to stay on farms; many keep livestock and have horses; some offer birdwatching excursions or fishing trips. Huts and cabins are ideal, too; depending on

Photo: Carriage ride at the Árbæjarsafn open-air museum

In the land of horses and trolls: how did the Vikings live; what are the whales up to? Iceland has answers to all these questions

the type, they offer plenty of space and often have their own kitchen. Many hotels and guest houses have special family rooms with up to six beds.

In the larger villages there are playgrounds at the campsites, and many swimming pools have special attractions for children, such as slides. Open-air museums offer kids plenty of room to make their own discoveries, especially *Skógar* in the South, *Glaumbær* in the North and *Hnjótur* in the West. Not surprisingly, the saga museums and reconstructed long-

houses, too, offer vivid and exciting encounters with the past.

You can undertake whale-watching excursions from many coastal villages; out at sea, you can learn a lot about the various species of this giant marine mammal. The dolphins are particularly curious, swimming up close to the boats. On walks, you're likely to come across free-roaming mother sheep with their lambs.

REYKJAVÍK

ÁRBÆJARSAFN (119 D5) (𝄞 E9)
At weekends, the open-air museum offers special children's activities, including courses in old agricultural practices. There is also an interesting exhibition of old toys. *June–Aug daily 10am–5pm | Kistuhylur 4 | Admission: 1000 ISK, children: free | www.arbaejarsafn.is*

Centre | Departure from Ægisgarður harbour | tel. 5 55 35 65 | 8000 ISK, children (7–15 years): 3500 ISK | www.elding.is

REYKJAVÍK PARK & ZOO (119 D5) (𝄞 E9)
This is the place to see Iceland's farm animals, as well as seals, greylag geese, reindeer, mink and Arctic fox. There's also a small fun park with carousels,

Flying start: on Heimaey, the local kids help young, stranded puffin chicks get back on track

VISIT THE ELVES (119 D5) (𝄞 E 9–10)
On a guided walk through Hafnarfjörður you'll be taken to the place the elves live. There's plenty to discover, especially in *Hellisgerði* park, such as caves and intriguingly shaped lava formations. Use your imagination and it becomes clear that they would make ideal elf 'houses'! The tour starts at the Tourist Information Office. *Tue/Fri 2.30pm | Hidden World Tours | tel. 6 94 27 85 | 3600 ISK incl. map; children: free | www.alfar.is*

BOAT TRIP (119 D4–5) (𝄞 E9)
Why not take a boat trip to have look at the thousands of puffins which live on the islands of Lundey and Akurey just off the coast near Reykjavík. *Whale Watching*

boats, miniature racetrack, a BMX course and much more. A restaurant rounds off the list of attractions. *15 May–Aug daily 10am–6pm, Sept–14 May daily 10am–5pm | Engjavegur | Admission: Mon–Fri 600 ISK, children (5–12 years): 500 ISK; Sat/Sun 700/600 ISK | www.husdyragardur.is*

Right next door is Reykjavík's *Botanical Garden*, a varied park landscape which is home to around 5000 species of plant, organised according to themes.

THE SOUTH

HEIMAEY (120 A6) (𝄞 G12)
In August, when the fledgling puffins take to the air, many stray into the small

town, attracted by the street lights and the noise. The local children round them up in the night and set them free again the following morning.

THE EAST

STEINASAFN PETRU (123 F2) (*M S7*)

For decades, Petra Sveinsdóttir has been putting together her impressive collection of stones which she has now lovingly arranged in her garden. It is often possible to come across unusual stones on walks in the East of Iceland. *Daily 9am–6pm or by arrangement | tel. 4 75 88 34 | Stöðvarfjörður Sunnuhlið | Admission: 500 ISK, children: free*

THE NORTH

SAFNAHÚSIÐ
(HÚSAVÍK MUSEUM) (115 F1) (*M M3*)

Much acclaimed for its natural-history display featuring a stuffed polar bear. This particular specimen was shot in 1969 on the island of Grimsey, having drifted there on an ice floe from Greenland. *June–Aug daily 10am–6pm, Sept–May Mon–Fri 9am–5pm, Sun 4pm–6pm | Stórigarður 17 | Admission: 600 ISK, children under 16: free | www.husmus.is*

HVAMMSTANGI (113 F5) (*M G–F 4–5*)

Around 35 km to the north of Hvammstangi on the west coast of the Vatnsnes Peninsula you are almost sure to be able to spot a few seals: their favourite places to sun themselves and have a rest are near Illugastaðir and Hindisvík. You can find out all about these animals at the INSIDER TIP *Icelandic Seal Center | Hvammstangi | Brekkugata 2 | June–Aug daily 9am–5pm | Admission: 900 ISK, children (6–16 years): 450 ISK | www.selasetur.is*

INSIDER TIP JÓLAGARÐURINN
(115 E3) (*M L4*)

If you love Christmas, don't miss a visit to the 'Christmas Garden', 5km/3mi south of Akureyri. You can buy Icelandic Christmas decorations and other seasonal items at the shop – and there's a café. *June–Aug daily 10am–10pm, Sept–Dec 2pm–10pm, Jan–May 2pm–6pm*

THE HIGHLANDS

LOOKING FOR TROLLS

Have you any idea why some blocks of lava look like human figures? It's because they were originally trolls which were turned to stone after failing to return to their caves before the sun came up! You can learn lots more about trolls in the picture book 'Icelandic Trolls' by Brian Pilkington, an Icelandic-British illustrator. The book also contains a map identifying the locations of the biggest and most striking trolls in Iceland. In the Highlands in particular, your children can meet many of these charming fellows! Incidentally, trolls are the cause of volcanic eruptions – when they are doing their cooking!

LANGJÖKULL
(120 A–B 1–2) (*M G–H 7–8*)

A ride in a dog-sled across the glacier is fun for everyone. The powerful Greenlandic huskies, the name of the breed used, just love racing across the ice. After the ride, you can even say thank you by giving them a friendly pat. If you book a whole day, you'll have the opportunity to learn how to steer a sled and try it out for yourself. In the evening, you get to feed the dogs, too. *Eskimo Travel | tel. 8 99 17 91 and 4 14 15 00 | www.dogsledding.is | from 1.5 hrs (14,900 ISK per person), up to whole day (45,000 ISK), children under 12 pay half price*

FESTIVALS & EVENTS

The Icelanders like to party – where possible, outside – with of course the obligatory masses of hearty food and fortifying drinks. The religious holidays are mostly celebrated within the family, with Christmas playing a special role. The 13 Father Christmases, or 'Yule Lads', – a really weird bunch – start to arrive on 12 December, bringing the children a small present every day. The first is the 'Sheep-Cote Clod', who leaves again on Christmas Day, and the last one is the 'Candle Stealer', arriving on Christmas Eve and returning to the mountains on 6 January, the 13th day of the Christmas period. What's more, it's traditional to dress up in something really smart on Christmas Eve – and it has to be something new, otherwise the Yule Cat will get you!

FESTIVALS & EVENTS

FEBRUARY

▶ *Carnival* in Iceland goes through the stomach: On Monday *(bolludagur)* it's cream-filled buns and on Shrove Tuesday *(sprengidagur)*, mountains of lamb and peas. On Ash Wednesday *(öskudagur)*, children in fancy dress collect sweets and money.

APRIL

The third Thursday is officially the ▶ *first day of summer* and street party time, whatever the weather – and snow is not uncommon in April!
In the same month, school-leavers take to Reykjavík's streets in costumes and high spirits!

MAY

The annual ▶ ★ *Reykjavík Arts Festival* showcases international and national artists from all genres. In recent years, other places have also taken part.

JUNE

To celebrate ▶ *Sailors' Day* on the first weekend of June, cultural and sporting events and markets take place in fishing villages all over the island.

A profusion of parties: silly Santas, sheep-sorting and summer in April

The high point is ▶ ⭐ *Independence Day* on 17 June. The official commemoration is on Austurvöllur square in the capital, where the President lays a wreath at the Jón Sigurðsson monument. The fjalla konan, the 'Lady of the Mountains', sings the praises of the country's beautiful landscape. The unofficial part is a huge street party.

AUGUST

The first weekend is a long one, thanks to the ▶ *bank holiday Monday*, traditionally a day for countryside trips. Heimaey, especially, is overrun with visitors, when Independence Day is celebrated again with rock concerts and firework displays. In early August, things get a little outrageous when crowds of gays and lesbians fill the streets for their ▶ *Gay Pride* parade.

On the third weekend, get your trainers on for ▶ *Reykjavík Marathon,* followed by ▶ INSIDERTIP *Culture Night* with a raft of concerts, readings and exhibitions –

all free of charge – and culminating in a firework display.

SEPTEMBER

Farmers on horseback set out to round up their herds of sheep in the Highlands. Back in the villages, they are driven into large pens *(réttur)* and then sorted. The end of this tiring and difficult task is celebrated with music, dancing and heaps of food. This ▶ ⭐ *rounding-up ritual* ritual attracts many foreign visitors who may also join in the ride.

OCTOBER

The annual ▶ *Film Festival* in Reykjavík features international and Icelandic pictures.

To experience mostly Icelandic musicians and bands, head for the ▶ *Iceland Airwaves Festival* which has bagged a fixed spot in the international alternative music calendar.

LINKS, BLOGS, APPS & MORE

LINKS

▶ www.samferda.is Free car-pooling service, ideal if you want to get from A to B and don't want to take the conventional hitch-hiking option. A contribution to petrol costs is customary

▶ www.eymundsson.is If you can't make it in person to Iceland's biggest and oldest bookstore (see also p. 37), visit their website which has a special visitors section in English. Good source of books on Iceland, CDs and DVDs, too, and the place to order your maps in advance

▶ www.grapevine.is Look no further than the aptly named Grapevine for details of what's happening in Reykjavík and indeed the whole island. Background articles, arts reviews, etc.

▶ www.travelnet.is Bags of information on accommodation, car hire, tour operators and even ideas for where to eat out in Iceland, including useful links

▶ www.icelandreview.com 'A window on Icelandic society', to quote its deputy editor, the Iceland Review (also in printed form) has news, reviews, features and events listings

VIDEOS & STREAMS

▶ www.sagenhaftes-island.is/en An initiative by the Icelandic Ministry of Culture, Education and Science, 'Fabulous Iceland' took the platform of the Frankfurt Book Fair in 2011, when Iceland was guest of honour, as an opportunity to showcase the country through its literature. The site also includes superb video portraits of writers and their relationship to their island heritage (with English subtitles)

▶ www.icelandair.co.uk While you're checking out the options for flying to Iceland (see also 'Travel Tips: Arrival') you should follow the link to the 'Unique Iceland' video. Take a tour of the island from the comfort of your armchair and savour the delights in store for you on your holiday

▶ www.inspiredbyiceland.com/ What do I love about Iceland? Follow this shortcut to under-

Regardless of whether you are still preparing your trip or already in Iceland: these addresses will provide you with more information, videos and networks to make your holiday even more enjoyable

stand what makes the island so fascinating. There are videos and music clips – some of which are also available on YouTube – and two webcams, one showing bathers at the Blue Lagoon and the other watching the birds on the Tjörnin lake in the middle of Reykjavík

▶ icelandeyes.blogspot.de Award-winning blog by a keen photographer. It's no surprise that her pictures – and the ones supplied by guest photographers – are a brilliant advertisement for a trip to Iceland. Scroll down the left for some links to breathtakingly beautiful videos, too

▶ www.ablogabouticeland.com What you see is what you get: a showcase on the people and places of the island and some fascinating travel diaries peppered with fantastic photos and video footage

BLOGS & FORUMS

▶ Reykjavík Walking Tours and Map Diverse sights in Reykjavík are presented, along with maps of themed city tours on subjects such as 'Museums', 'Shopping' or 'Nightlife'

▶ Lingopal Icelandic Talking phrase book for your travels, but maybe most suitable for adults, i.e. it won't be much use for families at the playground, but if you're stuck for a few chat-up lines in a downtown Reykjavík bar, this could help – guaranteed success is not part of the package, though

▶ Locatify Iceland Several tours for you to download and undertake under your own steam, such as the 'Golden Circle', 'Vikings in West Iceland' or a trip to the realm of the 'hidden people'

APPS

▶ www.virtualtourist.com Giant travel community with user-contributed reviews, videos, travel journals and tips. There's a forum for posting specific travel questions and a hotel-search function, too

▶ www.couchsurfing.org The Couchsurfers are a hospitality network on the Internet. If you're looking for a place to stay for free, take a look here. Incidentally, the couch-surfing idea was actually born in Iceland; the network founder e-mailed students at random during his time on the island and was amazed at the number of invitations he received

NETWORKS

TRAVEL TIPS

ACCOMMODATION

With the exception of Radisson SAS or Hilton you will only find Icelandic hotel chains on the island. There are, for example, seven Icelandair hotels offering luxury facilities *(www.icehotels.is)*. They are followed by the ten Foss hotels, often in very charming locations but unfortunately totally over-priced *(www.fosshotel.is)*. The 13 Edda hotels offer summer-time accommodation in boarding schools and colleges; many have a swimming pool, restaurant and their own bar, and the rooms have a shower and WC. A number of these hotels offer sleeping bag accommodation as an alternative *(www.hoteledda.is)*.

Icelandic Farm Holidays is an association of farms which provide not only accommodation but also a range of activities, such as riding, fishing, hunting, swimming and the chance to participate in the annual rounding-up of sheep from the summer pastures. Brochure and information: *Icelandic Farm Holidays (Reykjavík | Síðumúla 13 | tel. 5 70 27 00 | www.farmholidays.is)*. Some of the farms have cottages for rent. A number of tour operators rent out private summer cottages or holiday apartments, but these often have to be booked for a minimum of one week. Viator is one such company on the island *(www.viator.is)*.

Check out the site of travel guide publishers Heimur *(www.heimur.is/world)* and click on *áning* for lists of accommodation options according to region. The *www.accommodation.is* (Gisting) site is also a good source of ideas.

INSIDER TIP Affordable four-star stays are to be had if you book via the Internet, ideally outside the summer season. You might pick up an offer with up to 50 per cent discount on the regular price.

RESPONSIBLE TRAVEL

It doesn't take a lot to be environmentally friendly whilst travelling. Don't just think about your carbon footprint whilst flying to and from your holiday destination but also about how you can protect nature and culture abroad. As a tourist it is especially important to respect nature, look out for local products, cycle instead of driving, save water and much more. If you would like to find out more about eco-tourism please visit: *www.ecotourism.org*

ARRIVAL

Since Iceland has become such an immensely popular travel destination, the number of flights to the island has consequently risen. *Icelandair*, the oldest national carrier, flies from London. The price system is rather complicated, but it is possible to book reasonably priced flights by doing so early and flying outside the high season in summer. Be sure to compare offers from other airlines *(www.icelandair.is)*. The second Icelandic airline is *Iceland Express* which also departs from London. Flights are generally cheaper *(www.icelandexpress.com)*. Budget carrier Easyjet also offers connections from London *(www.easyjet.com)*. KLM flies from New York direct to Reykjavík, the trip taking around 6 hours *(www.klm.com)*. Look on the website of

From arrival to weather

Holiday from start to finish: the most important addresses and information for your trip to Iceland

Keflavík Airport for an up-to-date list of other carriers currently serving Reykjavík; in recent years these have been known to change frequently (www.kefairport.is).

You can take the ‚Norröna' ferry, operated by Smyril Line, to travel from Hirtshals (Denmark) to Seyðisfjörður. The ferry runs between April and October, and high season is from mid-June to mid-August. An interesting option for those wanting to explore Iceland with their own vehicle. www.smyril-line.com

BANKS & CURRENCY

Opening times: Mon–Fri 9.15am–4pm. You can withdraw cash using your credit card from the ATMs installed at most banks. The most widely used credit cards are Mastercard and Visa which are accepted nationwide.

The Icelandic currency is the króna (ISK). There are coins to the value of 1, 5, 10, 50 and 100 ISK as well as banknotes valued at 500, 1000, 2000 and 5000 ISK.

CAMPING

There are 150 campsites with various types of facilities, most of which are only open in the summer. Standards differ greatly, depending on the location: town/village or Highlands. On average you can expect to pay around 1600 ISK per person per night. With the INSIDER TIP Camping Card for 14900 ISK, you can pitch your tent on 42 sites. It is valid for two adults and up to four children (under 16 years of age). What's more, you can even have the card sent to your home address before embarking on

your holiday. www.campingcard.is Wild camping is not allowed in the vicinity of proper campsites, in National Parks and on farmed land, such as meadows and pasture.

CAR HIRE

Almost all larger places have a car-hire firm. It always pays to compare prices offered by the various companies; the smallest models cost around 12640 ISK per day in the summer. Hire cars are relatively new and suited to Icelandic driving

CURRENCY CONVERTER

£	ISK	ISK	£
1	188	2	0.01
3	564	10	0.05
5	940	25	0.13
13	2,444	80	0.43
40	7,520	150	0.80
75	14,100	500	2.67
120	22,500	1,200	6.40
250	47,000	10,000	53
500	94,000	50,000	267

$	ISK	ISK	$
1	120	2	0.01
3	362	10	0.08
5	600	25	0.21
13	1,570	80	0.66
40	4,800	150	1.25
75	9,000	500	4.15
120	14,440	1,200	10
250	30,000	10,000	83
500	60,000	50,000	416

For current exchange rates see www.xe.com

conditions. Drivers must be at least 20 years of age – for off-road vehicles, 23 – and have had a driving licence for at least one year. If you take your hire car into the Highlands or on rough, off-road trails, you will be fined accordingly. All costs arising from ensuing damage will be borne by the person hiring the vehicle.

CLIMATE, WHEN TO GO

The most popular time to travel to Iceland is from June to August, with the highest average temperatures hitting 13°C/55°F, the likelihood of rain at its lowest and the days are longest. An ideal holiday time is September, the only true autumnal month. At this time, when Iceland is cloaked in myriad golden hues, your chances of having the country – almost – to yourself are relatively good. In addition, the tradition of driving the sheep down into the valleys is celebrated in numerous festivals. Another good time to go is May, when the days are long and the first buds and blossoms are appearing. It's also the time for the *Reykjavík Art Festival*, and outdoor life gets under way in earnest. In the winter, it can get very cold on account of the wind; on the other hand, this is the best time for a sighting of the Northern Lights. Iceland is notorious for its changeable weather, so don't forget to pack your waterproofs and a warm jumper.

CONSULATES & EMBASSIES

UK EMBASSY
101 Reykjavík | Laufásvegur 31 | tel. 5505100 | info@britishembassy.is | ukiniceland.fco.gov.uk
US EMBASSY
101 Reykjavík | Laufásvegur 21 | tel. 5629100 | iceland.usembassy.gov

CUSTOMS

Adults may bring goods into Iceland duty- and tax-free as follows (in the case of alcohol, the minimum age is 20): 1 l alcohol up to 47 per cent, either 1 l of wine up to 21 per cent and 6 l of beer or 12 l beer, 200 cigarettes or 250 g of other tobacco products, foodstuffs up to 3 kg. It is prohibited to bring in animals, narcotics, fresh meat, fresh dairy products and eggs. Information under *www.tollur.is*
You are not permitted to take the following out of Iceland: plants, egg shells, birds' eggs, nests, birds, pieces of stone broken out of caves or any other protected monuments. Historical or archaeological artefacts may also not be exported.

DRIVING

The statutory speed limit in built-up areas is 50km/h (31mph), on overland roads with gravel surface 80km/h (50mph) and 90km/h (56mph) on asphalt. The loose gravel offers vehicles little grip, and you must be careful when swerving to avoid oncoming traffic on the often narrow roads. Warning signs with the word 'blindhæð' indicate blind rises crossing hills. Animals, such as free-roaming sheep, always have right of way in Iceland. It is compulsory to drive with dipped headlights, even during the day. All persons travelling in the vehicle must wear a seatbelt. The blood-alcohol limit is 0 per cent.
For driving in the Highlands, you'll need an off-road vehicle. In the summer, the Icelandic Road Administration (Vegagerðin), in collaboration with the Iceland Nature Conservation Association, issues a map which is updated every week showing which routes across the Highlands are open to traffic. If you drive on such a trail before it has been officially declared open, you can be fined; the police regularly monitor traf-

fic, also from the air. It is also strictly prohibited to drive outside the marked trails. Information: *www.vegagerdin.is*

Apart from in the Highlands, there is a fairly dense network of petrol stations. In Reykjavík and the larger towns, they are generally open until midnight. Here, you can often fill up and pay using 500- or 1000-ISK notes or credit card at self-service machines. Unleaded petrol (95 octane and 98 octane) as well as diesel *(dísel)* are available.

EMERGENCY SERVICES

Nationwide emergency telephone number: 112

HEALTH

In the event of serious illness or an accident, you should contact the A&E department *(slysadeild)* at a hospital *(sjúkrahús)* or contact a doctor *(læknir)* directly. Medical bills must be paid in cash. Find out from your medical insurance company before your travel which costs will be covered, and take out separate travel health insurance for your trip, if necessary.

Pharmacies *(apótek)* are recognisable by the sign with a cross and the words 'Lyf og heilsa'. They are open during normal business hours, and there is usually one on duty around the clock in Reykjavík. If you are dependent on regular medication, be sure to take a sufficient stock with you, in case it is not possible to obtain precisely the same products in Iceland.

HOSTELS

The 36 youth hostels are available to everyone and there are no age restrictions. Information, including brochures with descriptions of locations and facilities, is available from the youth hostel association *Bandalag Íslenska Farfugla* (Reykjavík | Borgartún 6 | tel. 5 75 67 00 | www.hostel.is).

IMMIGRATION

For travellers arriving from countries which have signed up to the Schengen Agreement, there is no passport control; others will of course be checked as normal. If you are bringing your own vehicle into

BUDGETING

Bus ride	5.60 $ / 3.60 £
	for a day ticket on Reykjavík's buses
Souvenir	from 125 $ / 80 £
	for an Icelandic pullover
Beer	from 5 $ / 3.20 £
	for 0.5 l in a bar
Coffee	from 3.10 $ / 2 £
	for two cups
Tomatoes	4.35 $ / 2.80 £
	for 1 kg home-grown
Swimming pool	3.75 $ / 2.40 £
	admission charge in Reykjavík

Iceland, you must carry your passport, vehicle registration documents, proof of valid insurance cover ('green card') and your driving licence. Drivers from the UK, US, Canada, Australia, New Zealand and most other European countries can use their standard licence; other drivers should check whether they have to apply for an international driving licence before leaving home.

INFORMATION

PRE-TRAVEL
Icelandic Tourist Office | 172 Tottenham Court Rd. | London W1P 9LG | tel. 171 3 88 55 99 | www.visiticeland.com

Icelandic Tourist Board in the USA | c/o The Scandinavian Tourist Board | 655

Third Avenue | New York, NY 10017 | tel. 212 8 85 97 00 | www.visiticeland.com
IN ICELAND
Ferðamálaráð Íslands | Geirsgata 9 | 101 Reykjavík | tel. 5 35 55 00 | www.visitice land.com

INTERNET & WLAN

– *www.iceland.is:* Iceland's official site, on which it showcases nature, culture and the economy. The comprehensive list of links is an excellent source of information.
– *www.visiticeland.com:* The official tourism website is packed with all the information you'd expect to find about what to see and do, where to stay and how to get around.
– *www.safetravel.is:* Run by Icelandic Search and Rescue, the site has useful information for the more adventurous Iceland visitor. Tips on equipment, road conditions, emergency procedures, etc.
– *www.nat.is:* Here, you'll find plenty of information, especially on rural Iceland, cross-country trails and all kinds of outdoor activities.

Icelanders are among the world's keenest Internet users, so it's no surprise to find hotspots in the large hotels – often in the entrance hall – and Internet access in rooms. If you are travelling without your laptop, you can often get on the Web at the tourist information offices.

MEDIA

From June to August, you can listen to the news in English every morning at

WEATHER IN REYKJAVÍK

	Jan	Feb	March	April	May	June	July	Aug	Sept	Oct	Nov	Dec
Daytime temperatures in °C/°F												
	2/36	3/37	5/41	6/43	10/50	13/55	15/59	14/57	12/54	8/46	5/41	4/40
Nighttime temperatures in °C/°F												
	–3/27	–3/27	–1/30	1/34	4/40	7/45	9/48	8/46	6/43	3/37	0/32	–2/29
Sunshine hours/day												
	1	2	4	5	7	5	7	6	4	3	2	1
Precipitation days/month												
	14	12	12	12	10	10	10	12	13	14	14	15
Water temperature in °C/°F												
	4/40	4/40	4/40	5/41	7/45	9/48	11/52	11/52	10/50	7/45	6/43	5/41

7.30am on 92.4/93.5 FM – in the day-time also by telephone under *tel. 5 15 36 90*. The BBC World Service broadcasts 24 hours a day on 90.9 FM.

International newspapers can be bought at larger bookshops in Reykjavík, usually one day after publication. Outside the capital you are less likely to find any. 'Grapevine' is a free English-language newspaper available at many outlets.

OPENING HOURS

Shops are open as follows: Mon–Fri 9am–6pm, Sat 10am–2pm (sometimes until 4pm). Some supermarkets are open until 11pm, 7 days a week. The *Kringlan* shopping centre in Reykjavík and Smáralind in Kópavogur have extended opening on Thursdays and open on Sundays (except in summer). Kiosks *(sjópa)* are usually open for business until 11.30pm, selling drinks and a small range of foods. Restaurants and also the tourist information offices are generally open every day.

PHONE & MOBILE PHONE

Telephone calls to Iceland: dial 00354, then the 7-digit number. Calling from Iceland: UK 0044, USA 001; then the area code without the 0.

GSM mobile phones can be used thanks to international roaming agreements. With the corresponding SIM card and the appropriate Icelandic telephone number, pre-paid cards can be purchased from the telephone service provider *Síminn* (information free of charge under *tel. 8 00 70 00*). You can also obtain them at service stations or kiosks. For the Highlands and some peripheral regions, you need to use phones operating under the Scandinavian NMT system.

If you want to use your phone a lot while in Iceland and would like to save on expensive roaming charges, it might be a good idea to hire a GSM mobile phone from Landssíminn *(Reykjavík | Ármúli 27)* and buy the appropriate pre-paid card.

POST

There are post offices *(póstur)* in all towns and larger villages. Opening times: Mon–Fri 8.30am–4.30pm. Air-mail letters and postcards up to 20 g within Europe cost from 140 ISK. *www.postur.is*

PRICES

Prices tend to be a good deal higher than the rest of Europe, not least due to the high rate of VAT, 25.5 per cent. Alcoholic beverages are particularly expensive.

In Iceland, tips and VAT are included in prices. There is an unfortunate trend, though, towards giving tips, although this is neither necessary nor expected.

PUBLIC TRANSPORT

Iceland has an extensive public bus network, and in the summer months several bus passes are on offer with reduced fares. You can get on and off at any point along the route. Information on tours, timetables, fares and special offers: *Destination Iceland (BSÍ bus station | www.bsi.is)*. Reykjavík has its own city bus network, operated by Strætó *(www.straeto.is)*.

Air Iceland and Eagle Air fly to various destinations in Iceland and also offer charter flights. The offers listed on the Internet are the cheapest. *Information: www.ernir.is and www.airiceland.is*

TIME

Iceland uses Greenwich Mean Time (GMT) all year round.

NOTES

ROAD ATLAS

The green line ▬▬▬ indicates the Trips & Tours (p. 84–89)
The blue line ▬▬▬ indicates the Perfect route (p. 30–31)

All tours are also marked on the pull-out map

Photo: Mývatn lake

Exploring Iceland

The map on the back cover shows how the area has been sub-divided

A

B

C

1

Kögur
Straumnes
Fannalágarfjall
Látrar
618
Horn
Aðalvík
Ritur
Sæból
Hesteyri
Lækjarfjall
Ísafjarðardjúp
Lókulfjörður

2

Skálavík • 13
Öskubakur
Keflavík
517
Svartafjall
Bolungarvík
15
Suðureyri
Miðdalur
Hnífsdalur
Súgandafjörður
Staður
724
Ísafjörður
Flateyri
5 3
17
Vigur
Kambsnes
Önundarfjörður
Sæból
Kirkjuból
Súðavík
Hesti
Hvítanes
Fjallaskagi
624
678
Holt
Breiðdalsheiði
566

3

Þverfell
60
Korpudalur
61
Núpur
45
Hattardalur
957
Lambadalsfjall
Dýrafjörður
Mýrar
15
Botnss
Heydal
Svalvogar
Hraun
622
Þingeyri
9
Gláma
920
Haukad.
Lokinhamrar
998
Hjálkárvirkjun
Hrafnabjörg
Kaldbakur
9
Kópur
458
619
Álftamýri
17
Vestfi
Selárdalur
Hrafnseyri
15
Grænahlíð
Arnarfjörður
Langanes
Borgarfjörður
10
Stóra-Eyjavatn
Fremrivesta
26
Dynjandi
Bíldudalur
60
Dynjandisheiði
Stóri-Laugardalur
Trastansfj.
Þingmannaheiði
Tálknafjörður
63
Vatnsfjörður
Vattar

4

Blakknes
Tálknafjörður
15
13
63
8
60
Kollsvík
617
28
36
23
706
Hænuvík
615
62
Patreksfjörður
Miðvörðurheiði
Flókalundur
42
Breiðavík
612
13
Vesturbotn
Birkimelur
Kefilngarfjörður
Hvallátur
Hnjótur
16
Hagi
Skálmarnesmúli
441
Sauðlauksdalur
614
12
Kleifaheiði
Brjánslækur
5
Innri Múli
61
Látrabjarg
10
Saurbær
13
Brekkuvellir
15
Saúðeyjar
Melanes
Hreggsstaðir
Barðaströnd
Rauðasandur
• 663
Skor
Hergilsey
Hvallátur
Svefney

11

Oddbjarnarsker
Flatey

5

Bjarneyjar

B r e i ð a f j ö r ð u r

Elliðaey
Arne

6

Höskuldsey

20 km
12.43 mi

Stykkishólmur
10
Skjöldur
58
Bjarnarhöfn
Helgafell
54
Setberg
576
Stöð
B4ulandshöfði
54 268 453
Kirkjufell
Bersekja
hraun
56
23
118
112
Hellissandur
Rif
Grundarfjörður
60
Gufuskálar
22

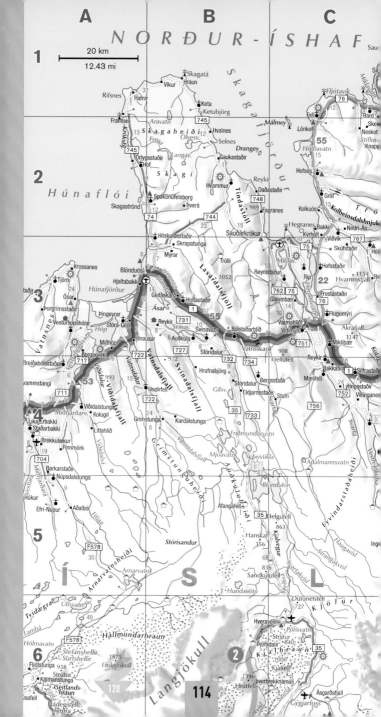

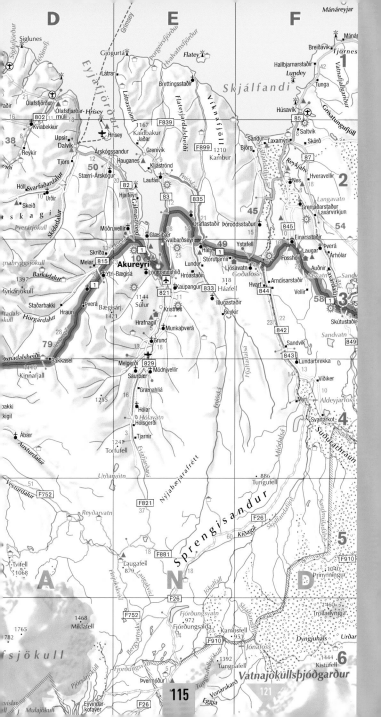

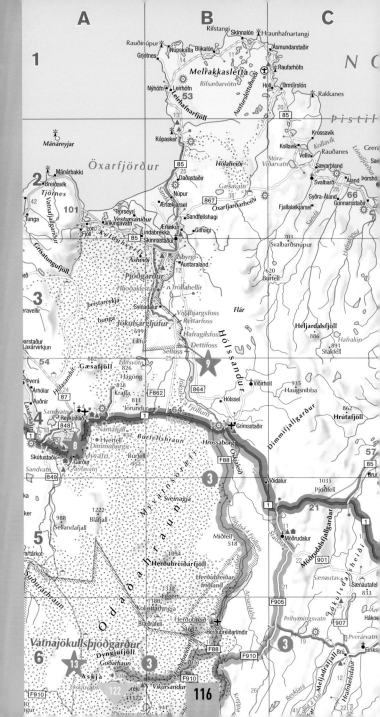

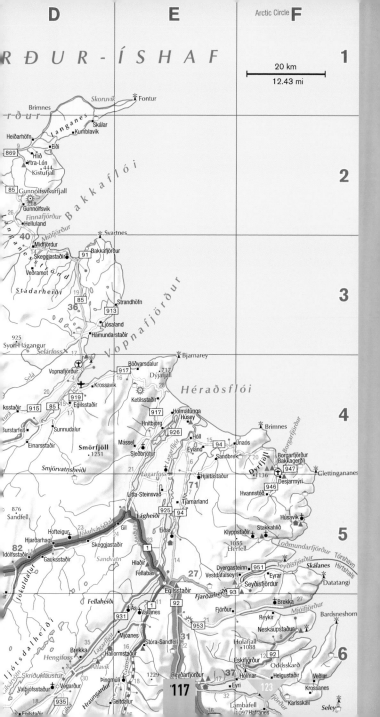

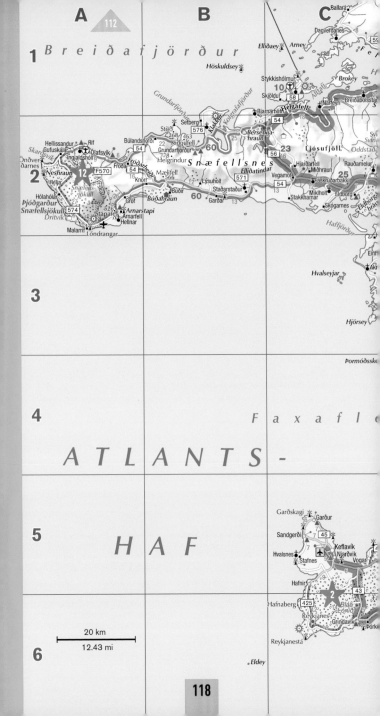

A ▲ 112 **B** **C**

1 *B r e i ð a f j ö r ð u r*

Ballará
Dagverðanes
Elliðaey Arney
Höskuldsey
Stykkishólmur **10** Brokey
Skjöldur **58** Narfeyri Breiðabólsstað
Grundarfjörður Bjarnarhöfn Helgafell **54**
2 Hellissandur Rif Búlandshöfði Setberg **576** Berserkja- Svi
Gufuskálar Ólafsvík Stöð **268** **463** **hraun** **23** Ljósufjöll Svína
Önver- Ingjaldshóll **54** Kirkjufell **60** Hjarðarfell Miðhraun Rauðamelur
ðarnes **F570** Fróðá Grundarfjörður **171** Vegamót Faskrúðarbakki **25**
Neshraun Fróðárheiði Helgrindur *S n æ f e l l s n e s* **571** **54** Miklholt Eldborg
12 Mælifell **12** Lýsuhóll **13** Stakkhamar Skógarnes
Snæfells- Knörr Staðarstaður
jökull Grof Búðir **60** Garðar **13**
Hólahólar *Búðahraun*
Þjóðgarður **574** Stapafell Arnarstapi
Snæfellsjökull Arnarfell
Dritvík Hellnar
Malarrif Löndrangar *Hafjörður*

3 Hvalseyjar Einr
Akl

Hjörsey

Þormóðsske

4 *F a x a f l e*

A T L A N T S -

5 Garðskagi Garður
Sandgerði **45**
H A F Hvalsnes Keflavík
Stafnes Njarðvík Vogar
Hafnir
Hafnaberg **425** **2** **43**
Blá
Lónið
Reykjanes Grindavík Þorka
Reykjanesta

6 20 km
12.43 mi Eldey

118

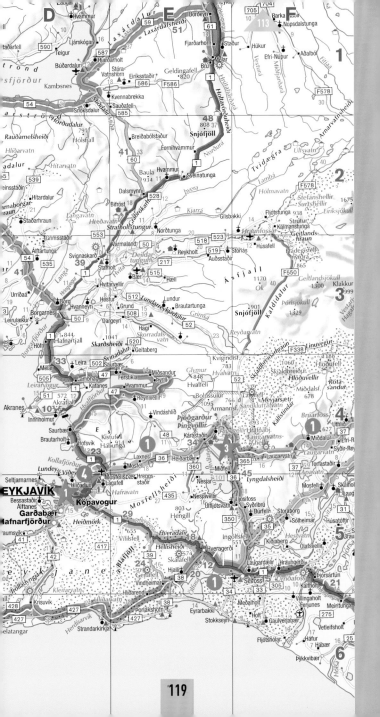

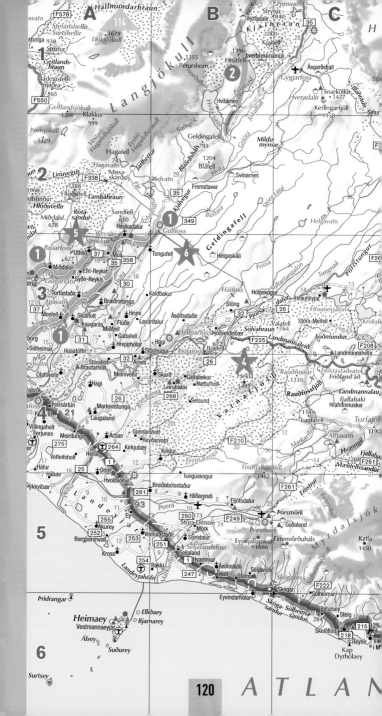

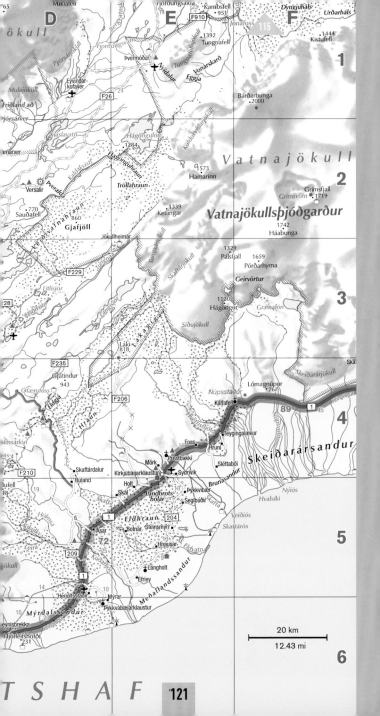

KEY TO ROAD ATLAS

Durchgangsstraße - Wichtige Hauptstraße		Thoroughfare - Important main road
Hauptstraßen - Nebenstraße		Main roads - Secondary road
Straßen, geschottert		Roads graveled
Fahrweg (nur bedingt befahrbar) - Fußweg		Carriageway (use restricted) - Footpath
Mautstelle - Furt - Pass - Wintersperre	✕ ⚡ XII–IV	Toll station - Ford - Pass - Closure in winter
Straßennummern	18 F45 63	Road numbers
Kilometrierung	19 14 7 23	Distances in km
Autofähre - Schifffahrtslinie		Car ferry - Shipping route
Verkehrsflughafen - Regionalflughafen - Flugplatz - Landeplatz	✈ ✈ ⊕ ✈	Airport - Regional airport - Airfield - Runway for aeroplanes
Sehenswert: Kultur - Natur	∗ Glaumbær ∗ Dimmuborgir	Of interest: culture - nature
Landschaftlich schöne Strecke - Touristenstraße		Route with beautiful scenery - Tourist route
Aussichtspunkt	☼	Point of view
Kirche - Kloster - Burg, Schloss - Ruinen	♁ ♁ ♁ ♪ ♪ ♪	Church - Monastery - Castle, palace - Ruins
Denkmal - Höhle - Wasserfall	▲ ∩ ⌒	Monument - Cave - Waterfall
Nationalpark - Naturpark		National park - Nature park
Jugendherberge - Campingplatz	▲ ▲	Youth hostel - Camping site
Berghütte - Rettungshütte	⌂ ⌂	Refuge - Emergency shelter
Allein stehendes Hotel	⌂	Isolated hotel
Vulkan	•	Volcano
Hauptstadt	**REYKJAVÍK**	Capital
Gletscher		Glacier
Ausflüge & Touren		Trips & Tours
Perfekte Route		Perfect route
MARCO POLO Highlight	★	MARCO POLO Highlight
Lava		Lava

Lava area © Icelandic Institute of Natural History

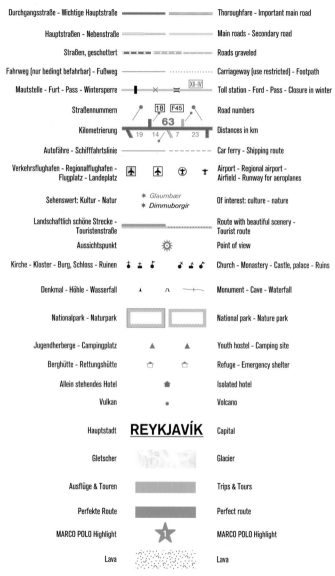

INDEX

This index lists all places, destinations and important personalities mentioned in the guide, as well as a few other concepts. Page numbers in bold type refer to the main entry.